CB 448

JAGUAR Mk 2 SALOONS

2·4, 3·4 & 3·8-LITRE

Paul Skilleter

CONTENTS

ISBN 0 85429 307 8

A FOULIS Motoring Book

First published 1982
Reprinted 1982, 1987

© **Haynes Publishing Group**

Published by:
Haynes Publishing Group,
Sparkford, Nr Yeovil,
Somerset BA22 7JJ

Haynes Publications Inc.
861 Lawrence Drive, Newbury
Park, California 91320, USA

Editor: Rod Grainger
Dust jacket design: Rowland
Smith
Printed in England by:
J.H. Haynes & Co. Ltd

Further titles in this series will be published at regular
intervals. For information on new titles please contact
your bookseller or write to the publisher.

FOREWORD

Just as this book closed for press, John Egan, Chairman and Managing Director of Jaguar Cars Ltd, stated publicly the company's firm intention to produce once more a "compact Jaguar", to be sold alongside the already scheduled XJ replacement. At present such a car is in the earliest of planning stages, but the fact that Jaguar have acknowledged the vital role which a small, sporting saloon could play in its future model range indicates once more the value and 'rightness' of the Mk 2 Jaguar saloon in its own time.

For many people, the Mk 2 was the ideal car. It wasn't too big, yet it was quite roomy enough for a family tour of a continent. It wasn't too thirsty, yet it had more performance than virtually any other saloon car on the road. There was no ostentation about its appearance, but it was handsome and distinctive. And, of course, while the quality was maintained, the on-the-road price was amazingly small when you considered all that your money bought. No wonder then, when Jaguar finally worked through the waiting lists for the XJ6, that the lack of a smaller, more economical and handier Jaguar saloon was felt in an age when the car buying public — even in the luxury bracket — had come to be a little shy of larger and thirstier vehicles.

In this book, the reader is given a comprehensive profile of the Mk 2 Jaguar, how it came about, what made it a success, and why it finally had to leave production. And while the car remained substantially unchanged over its 10-year lifespan (including the 240), there's a very detailed cataloguing of many of the minor improvements which Jaguar did incorporate in that period.

I would very much like to acknowledge the help of a few key people who contributed to this book. Firstly, Nigel Thorley who not only submitted to a formal interview for our "Owner's View", but also divulged many details about early Mk 2s, of which his own car, 7555 EL, must be one of the best and most original examples in existence. Nigel spent hours tracking down and confirming production changes and generally assisting me with this project.

I'm also very grateful to the other owners who put their magnificent cars at my disposal for a long photographic session, Ronald Andrews with his superb concours-winning dark blue 3.8, and R.W.B.Redcliffe whose golden-sand 3.4 must be about the best of its type in the country. Then I don't know what I would have done but for Karen Miller, who was able to supply much needed pictures of the North American specification Mk 2. Karen could not provide a Mk 2 from her or Ed Miller's stable (they have supreme examples of 'E' type and XK 120) but found what was required in the form of airline pilot Joe Rowe's lovely white 3.8 automatic. It isn't really necessary to say much more — the cars speak for themselves through the pictures, and add so much to the worth of this book.

Autocar and *Motor* magazines were extremely helpful in allowing the reproduction of their respective contemporary road tests of the Jaguar Mk 2.

Finally, I would like to thank Andrew Whyte for helping me out with pictures of the Mk 2 in competition, and Jaguar Cars themselves for photographs which filled in the gaps from my own collection. The end result has been, I hope, a compact yet comprehensive study of a car which, though it had its faults, is remembered with affection. I certainly enjoyed my ownership of a 3.8 Mk 2, and consider that a well-maintained example of the breed still represents an efficient, enjoyable and rapid means of covering long distances.

Paul Skilleter

HISTORY

Family tree

Particularly since the demise of the Mark 2, Jaguars are thought of as large cars, but the first true car which William Lyons and his partner William Walmsley built — the S.S.1 of 1931 — was definitely only "medium-sized", even by British standards. Indeed Lyons virtually began his career by rebodying the smallest British production car, the famous Austin Seven; it was only later on that S.S. Cars Ltd (which grew from the Swallow Coachbuilding Company) became associated with large, heavy designs.

The first true Jaguar appeared at the end of 1935, when the S.S.1 (which was really more of a two-plus-two than a saloon) was replaced by a roomy four-seater powered by a 2½-litre engine with a completely new overhead valve cylinder head developed by West Country expert Harry Weslake. This gave the SS Jaguar, with its stylish new coachwork, a superb performance in its class, and 90mph could be seen on the big speedometer with a minimum of help from wind or gradient.

Then alongside the ohv models was a further new Jaguar, powered by the sidevalve Standard engine of 1608cc which S.S. had

used in the S.S.1's smaller sister, the S.S.2. The "1½-litre" SS Jaguar was to be the smallest Jaguar ever produced, with a 9ft wheelbase and 13ft 11ins length. It had a scaled-down version of the 2½-litre saloon's styling and was even better value for money, at an astonishing £285 — some £23 cheaper than the 1½-litre Riley from the much older company just down the road from S.S. Cars' factory at Foleshill, Coventry.

During 1937/38, a new range of SS Jaguars replaced these cars, using a larger, all-steel body to speed production; a powerful 3½-litre ohv engine was added to the range, but a "1½-litre" model, using an ohv 1776cc engine in the same chassis (which had been designed by S.S. Cars' chief engineer William Heynes), continued Lyons' theme of offering a smaller-engined Jaguar for those who wanted the same comfort but didn't need the extra speed. The shrewd use of a common bodyshell and chassis enabled Lyons to sell the "1½-litre" for a ridiculous figure — around cost-price in fact. He sold lots of them too, and thus brought down the unit cost of components used for the 2½ and 3½-litre saloons on which a very healthy profit *was* made!

All three saloons, and their drophead variants, were put back into production after the war; but when the next new Jaguar saloon was announced, in 1948, a "small" engined Jaguar was missing — the MkV, with its new torsion bar independent-front-suspension chassis, was only offered with the 2½ and 3½-litre power units. Weight had gone up, and it seems that the 1.8 Standard engine just wouldn't have given an acceptable performance by post-war standards. Also, the 1.8's tooling was still owned by Standard, though Lyons had managed to buy the machinery which made the two larger power units.

The Mk V was a success, although it was rather

overshadowed by the astonishing XK120 launched at about the same time and which introduced Jaguar's new twin-cam XK engine. This magnificent 3.4-litre unit was seen within two years in the MkV's successor, the big, bulky MkVII saloon which used the same chassis and suspension. So Jaguar's range for 1951 (after the last MkVs were sold) consisted of just the XK120 and the MkVII. A "small" Jaguar appeared to have been forgotten.

In reality though, it certainly hadn't been forgotten. The XK engine, developed largely during the war years by Heynes, Hassan and Baily, was designed almost from the outset to be built in two sizes — a "six" and a "four". This was because Jaguar specifically intended to build a "small" saloon car as part of their postwar new-model programme, but the expense and work involved in getting the MkVII into production, and to a certain extent the meeting of the unforeseen demand for the XK120, ensured that work on the small car never seriously began. The 2-litre four-cylinder version of the twin-cam engine was offered in the XK120 initially, but the lure of 120mph from the larger 3.4 unit's 160bhp proved too great for the (mainly American) customer and no four-cylinder "XK 100s" were ever made.

Delayed it might have been, but the "small-Jaguar" project was not shelved as the reasons for making such a car remained valid. Just as for the pre-war 1½-litre model, sales volume was the goal: after all, a smaller car could be sold more cheaply and thus attract more customers. The MkVII could never meet this need for, while it offered superb value for money, it was undeniably large and way beyond the pocket of all but the well-off. When the MkVII was finally sorted-out for production, attention was at last turned to a smaller Jaguar.

The result was, of course, the 2.4-litre saloon which made its bow in September 1955. While there was a discernible family resemblance to the XK sports car in the treatment of its front end, and to the MkVII in the way the roof and tail were styled, it represented a distinct departure from tradition for Jaguar as it was the company's first venture into unitary-construction. This was new ground to Jaguar's body engineers who, after being given essential dimensions by Heynes and overall styling by Lyons, had to produce a "chassis-less" car in conjunction with the Pressed Steel Company's engineers who were based at Oxford. Jaguar's resources were still limited — it was, after all, a small company producing only around 6,000 cars a year. The new saloon taxed these resources to the utmost, both financially and in terms of experience and manpower; but the end result was a major success.

Besides its novel bodyshell, a new coil-spring front suspension arrived with the 2.4, together with a fresh approach to the rear suspension which used a cantilevered axle. It might have been powered by an engine entirely new to production as well, but plans to employ the four-cylinder version of the XK engine were dropped in favour of a shorter-stroke variant of the existing "six" which reduced its capacity to 2483cc. Rationalisation — the 2.4 used the same cylinder head as the 3.4 — and smoothness won the day here, and the 2-litre engine lost its last chance to power a production Jaguar.

Export was as vital to Jaguar then as it is today, and fortunately the new "compact" was well received in the United States, the company's most important overseas market. The only trouble was, people (especially American enthusiasts) kept asking why the larger 3.4 engine wasn't fitted — Jaguar had overestimated the appeal of economy over performance, and the average

American purchaser turned out to be far keener on impressive horsepower figures than a modest thirst for petrol. So, in 1957, along came the Jaguar 3.4-litre saloon, powered by the full 210bhp MkVIII engine and capable of staggering acceleration even by American standards — while, in Great Britain, only the XK150 and a handful of specialist sports cars were capable of staying with it in a straight line.

With the 3.4 saloon (£1,672), the cheaper-still 2.4 (£1,431) and the MkVIII replacement for the MkVII (£1,830), Jaguar had a very complete and near-ideal saloon car range, supplemented by the profitable but low-volume sports cars — by 1957 the XK150 in fixed-head, drophead and (within two years) open two-seater forms. Thanks largely to the compacts, production leapt from 9,900 cars in 1955 to 20,876 by the end of 1959, with profits well over the million-pound mark for the first time. Things looked good for Jaguar as the 'sixties approached . . . .

Introduction of the Jaguar Mk 2 Saloon

There was no complacency at Browns Lane, however, near the village of Allesley where the company had moved at the beginning of the 'fifties. The 2.4 and 3.4 had been highly successful but they were not without their shortcomings — the thickness of the window and door pillars had been criticised as "clumsy", and the velocities obtained by the 3.4-litre car in particular had demonstrated that handling, while safe, could be improved with advantage! These points and more were taken into consideration by Jaguar, and the net result was a much-revised version of the car, named simply the "Mark 2". The Mk 2 was, of course, to become one of Jaguar's best-loved and

most successful saloon cars, whose performance both on the road and in the sales charts has only been exceeded by one other Jaguar — the XJ6.

Rarely in the world of motor cars does a "facelift" improve (rather than merely modernise) an existing model, but Lyons' re-translation of the original "Mk 1" (as the earlier car immediately became known when the Mk 2 appeared) was nothing less than a triumph. While most of the original dimensions remained the same, the Mk 2 (introduced in October 1959) had a fresher, lighter look about it. This was mainly due to the big increase in glass area, beginning with a deeper (16½ins) windscreen matched by deeper and wider side windows. The effect had been achieved through thinner windscreen pillars, while the door window frames, formerly part of the door pressings, were replaced entirely by delicate, chrome-plated items which were bolted to the door shell. This type of separate window frame had been pioneered by American makes during the early forties, and Lyons himself — along with Alec Issigonis and his Morris Minor! — had introduced them to the British market with the coming of the MkV in 1948. He'd used them on the MkVII, VIII and XK fixed-heads as well; now they were incorporated, with great effect, on the new Mk 2.

Few changes were immediately obvious at the front of the car, though some had been made — the spotlights were positioned where the Mk 1's dummy air-intake grilles had been, and the sidelights were now on top of the wings a la the XK and MkIX cars. The radiator grille was new as well, now having a thick central rib in addition to the row of thin slats.

Inside, the car was virtually all new, with the Mk 2 becoming the first production Jaguar to have its main instruments — rev-counter and speedometer — set right in front of the driver, with supplementary instruments being contained in panel set in the centre of the fascia.

As for motive power, the Mk 2 range used three engine sizes — 2.4, 3.4 and 3.8. The less-exciting 2.4-litre engine was basically as used in the Mk 1 but power had been raised from 112bhp to 120bhp through the use of the B-type cylinder head; two Solex carburettors were still specified. Increased weight meant, however, that even with the additional bhp the car couldn't quite manage the two-way 100mph maximum of its predecessor, and Jaguar were careful not to loan the motoring press a 2.4 Mk 2 because, by that time, a Jaguar which couldn't manage 100mph might have been seen as something of a letdown! Although beautifully smooth and providing a perfectly adequate performance, the 2.4 engine did not offer that much in the way of extra economy over the larger units, so drivers turned to the 3.4 or 3.8 — which indeed were the only variants officially exported to such markets as the United States. However, some 25,000 2.4 Mk 2s *were* built, which wasn't that far short of a third of the Mk 2's entire production.

The 3.4 Mk 2 used Jaguar's familiar 3442cc engine in a similar state of tune to the original 3.4's, featuring the B-type cylinder head — this had supplemented the original XK head from 1957 on the introduction of the MkVIII and XK150 cars, and had larger (1⅝ instead of 1 5/16ins) exhaust valves and Jaguar's "high lift" (⅜ins) camshafts as standard, plus revised porting. This engine was rated at 210bhp and gave the car an almost 120mph top speed though, due again to the extra weight of the new model, it was a little slower on acceleration than the "old" 3.4.

The 3.8 Mk 2 was an even faster car, thanks to a capacity that was new to the Jaguar compact. Its 3781cc engine was

taken from the big MkIX saloon, the final expression of the MkVII series and itself no sluggard, winding-up to almost 115mph given the time. In the much lighter (30cwt) Mk 2 shell, the quoted 220bhp of the 3.8 engine produced an astonishing rate of progress for a luxury, four-seater, saloon car: virtually no other catalogued saloon, anywhere in the world, could match the 3.8's acceleration or top speed.

The small but vital increase in capacity over the original 3442cc came from taking the diameter of the bores from 83 to 87mm; this sort of thing had been done before by private owners for racing purposes simply by boring the existing block, but as this was inclined to produce cracking between the cylinders, Jaguar redesigned the block and used dry liners. As with the 3.4, the B-type cylinder head and two 1¾ins SU carburettors were used, an electric pump bringing fuel from the petrol tank in the car's tail.

Two basic types of transmission were available for all the Mk 2 range — a three-speed Borg Warner Type DG automatic gearbox, and a four-speed manual gearbox. Overdrive was an optional extra on the latter and, on the 3.4 and 3.8 cars, gave superbly long-legged cruising with its 2.933 gearing. A Powr-Lok differential by Thornton was standard on home-market 3.8s, and optional on North American vehicles; the 3.8 really needed it too, especially in the wet when the ample power available (and the rubber of the day) readily produced wheelspin, particularly from the inside wheel on acceleration out of a corner.

The Mk 2's suspension was very similar to the Mk 1's, with most of the novelty being at the rear. Here the live rear axle was suspended from the *ends* of two leaf springs, which were anchored at their centres inside an open channelling underneath the rear seat pan. The idea of this cantilever arrangement was to

reduce stress on the rear part of the bodyshell, and dates back to the original design of the 2.4 Mk 1 when unitary construction was new to Jaguar, and no chances were being taken of "under-engineering" the new body. Further location of the axle was provided by two trailing arms which ran from the rear bulkhead to rubber-mounted brackets above the axle casing, and an adjustable Panhard rod. It was all rather reminiscent of the C-type Jaguar's rear suspension, though the competition car used a transverse torsion bar.

The front suspension was more conventional but carefully thought-out. For instance, along with the steering box, it was mounted on a big, strong subframe; this was bolted to the car's shell by rubber mountings and thus dramatically cut down the amount of road noise transferred to the body. Possibly the only disadvantage of this arrangement was the necessity to drop the subframe complete with suspension every time the sump had to be taken off — but with a Jaguar engine that wasn't often required.

The suspension itself used two wishbones to carry a stub-axle and hub which incorporated typical Jaguar ball-joints; the bottom forged wishbone contained a pan for the coil spring, whose upper mounting was up inside the turret on which the shorter top wishbone pivoted; the telescopic damper ran inside the coil spring. An anti-roll bar connected the two lower wishbones. Much of the chassis design and development was carried out by R.J.(Bob) Knight, who was becoming one of the world's foremost engineers in the field of suspension and noise insulation.

Experience had quickly proved that the 3.4 saloon had been much too fast and heavy for drum brakes when its full performance was used, despite the factory's genuine belief that owners wouldn't drive it that fast! So, like most of the later 3.4s, all the Mk 2s were equipped with servo-assisted disc brakes. These were generally up to the performance of the car, at least on the road as opposed to the race track. The optional wire wheels, besides looking smart, aided brake cooling and were almost always used by competition drivers.

Like all its other major components, the Mk 2's bodyshell dated back substantially to the Mk 1 saloons, and indeed virtually all the non-exterior pressings were shared with the earlier car; it was this economy in tooling costs which both enabled Jaguar to sell the Mk 2 at such a competitive price, and almost certainly prevented the use of an even wider-track rear axle which the engineers might have desired. As it was, the Mk 1's particularly narrow rear track was increased for the Mk 2, but only by three inches or so.

When the car was built, the painted body was lowered onto the suspension, engine and transmission which would be positioned on a moving track underneath; on the 2.4 even the carburettors could be left on the engine, but the SUs of the other two variants had to be taken off while this procedure was carried out. The car was then moved on to the trim line for most of the interior to be installed, which would be followed by road-testing and final inspection before the completed car was sent to the despatch bay.

The Mk 2 changed very little during its production life, and the first and last examples would be difficult to tell apart — inside or out — if placed side by side. That was, of course, a key factor in the success of the car — firstly Lyons had got the formula pretty well correct right from the start, so it didn't *need* changing, and secondly, a long production run with few alterations meant that the maximum value was extracted from the tooling which enabled the

car's price to be kept down. And it was the Mk 2's exceptional value for money that helped keep it in production for so long.

Perhaps the first significant change to the car's specification didn't arrive until September 1965, when at last the Mk 2 gained an all-synchromesh gearbox; this could still be obtained with overdrive attached if desired, and made the Mk 2 considerably more pleasant to drive thanks to the reduced lever travel, and stronger synchromesh which now also featured on first gear. Perhaps this was the last *improvement* to the model as well, excepting the option of Varamatic power-steering, for thereafter the Mk 2 suffered from a cheapening process which to many people had spoilt much of its appeal by the end. In September 1966, Ambla upholstery replaced the leather seat facings, and the foglamps were replaced by dummy vents, as used on American export Mk 2s. But just before the Mk 2 became technically obsolete, Varamatic steering was offered which, with its variable ratio, was certainly an improvement on the previous type, reducing the ratio to under three turns of the steering wheel lock-to-lock.

The Mk 2 in perspective

The Mk 2 Jaguar was introduced in October 1959, to coincide with the London Motor Show. It was an auspicious year for new British cars, with important new models from Ford (the 105E Anglia) and Triumph (the all-independently-sprung Herald). But amongst the big cars, the latest Jaguar stood out as a brilliant new model despite its similarity to the previous 2.4 and 3.4. The 3.8 engined car, in particular, intrigued the motoring press and public alike with its promise of tremendous performance; this soon being

fulfilled when independent road-tests recorded acceleration times which put most sports cars to shame. There was simply no comparable closed car which could get near the 3.8 Mk 2 on outright performance, and even something like an Aston Martin DB4 (more of a GT sports car than a saloon) could only just match its 0-60mph and standing ¼-mile times (of 8.5 and 16.3 seconds respectively), though it was faster at the top end. If you brought price into the equation, then there was no contest at all — the Aston retailed at £3,755 in October 1959, the 3.8 Mk 2 £1,779 (though extras like overdrive or automatic transmission would just about bring it up to the £2,000 mark).

The car was slightly less competitively priced in the USA, where the 3.8 sold for about $5,000; but, again, it was hailed as a true "sports sedan" with old-English luxury thrown in. Roughly, it equated with such cars as the latest ($3,696) Ford Thunderbird in concept, the makers of which had stopped pretending they were building a sports car and had standardised on four seats from 1958, though the Jaguar with its 107ins wheelbase was considerably smaller than the "T-bird's" 113ins.

But it was in handling and general response on the road that really separated the Mk 2 from any potential American counterpart — it was simply streets ahead thanks to its sensible size and a suspension system that worked properly. The latter also provided an excellent ride, which again came as a surprise to an American driver new to a Jaguar. Understeer was the Mk 2's predominant handling characteristic, mainly due to some 57% of the car's weight being over the front wheels, but this was not excessive and made it a very safe car to "chuck about". The steering was probably the least impressive of the Mk 2's dynamic qualities, having almost five turns lock-to-lock even when the optional power assistance was specified, and it was followed closely by the gearbox whose origins could be traced back to at least the 1940s. The movement of the lever was long, the synchromesh was easily beaten, and the change was slow if it was to be kept silent. The box *was* tough and reliable though.

By absolute standards the Mk 2 was a low-volume production car, and it was never exactly a *common* sight in North America; but its looks and performance gained it a couple of "Best Imported Car" awards and a good deal of respect amongst the small proportion of American motorists who paid any attention to foreign cars (except VW Beatles) in those days. If you had to give up your XK150 or 'E' type because of a growing family, a Mk 2 saloon was an excellent substitute.

This line of reasoning applied in Great Britain too, though in addition many who would never have dreamed of buying a sports car purchased a Mk 2. The blend of elegance, near-devastating acceleration, an effortless three-figure cruising speed and a comparatively low initial cost made the car irresistible to those shopping for distinctive four-seater transport around the £2000-bracket. It was an ideal car for the Managing Director of a small company (or a large one come to that), the businessman with many miles to travel, the sporting motorist who wanted a comfortable saloon that wouldn't look silly at a weekend hillclimb or sprint meeting — or even the better-off retired couple who didn't favour the expense or bulk of the MkIX or X Jaguar.

The End of Production

The Mk 2 didn't so much cease production as fade away, for while the model name as such died in September 1967, the bodyshell continued for another 19 months in the shape of the slim-bumpered 240 and 340 Jaguars. Pleasant though they were, they never quite had the same charisma as the "proper" Mk 2, and were themselves distinctly old-fashioned by the time the last 240 left the factory in April 1969.

The phrase "old-fashioned" sums up why the Mk 2 itself finally left production; while its straight-line performance certainly hadn't dated, its heavy steering, handling and ride no longer came up to Jaguar's standards, and it was the S-type Jaguar — Mk 2 based but with longer rear end, remodelled front, and MkX-type independent rear suspension — that pointed the way ahead. In a way it is perhaps surprising that the Mk 2 (in 240 form) lasted as long as it did, overlapping the production of the superb XJ6 which stunned the motoring world with its refinement, silence and handling.

Having had a rather confusing array of models — besides the Mk 2, MkX, and S-type, the 'E' type was still in production, and the 420, another Mk 2 variant with the 4.2 engine, had appeared in October 1966 — Jaguar then put all its saloon-car eggs in the XJ basket. Had the company been able to foresee the various oil crises which were on the horizon, and the resulting increases in the price of petrol, possibly they might have considered producing a true Mk 2 replacement as well, of the type so badly needed by Jaguar today. As it is, the six and twelve-cylinder Jaguars remain top of their class, but as any enthusiast will tell you, they are in no way successors to the Mk 2. That car retains a unique place in Jaguar history, and in the hearts of Jaguar enthusiasts the world over.

The Mk 2 in Competition

On the race-track, the 3.8 Mk 2 rapidly established itself as about the only other saloon car which could vanquish the 3.4 Mk 1! Hardly a lightweight, the combination of good handling and an excellent output of power and torque from the trusty XK engine nevertheless proved virtually unbeatable for a number of years. The most important sphere of operations for the Mk 2 in this context was Europe, which was second only to the USA as an export market for Jaguar — so it was well worth the factory encouraging anyone who could stimulate sales by defeating such as Mercedes and BMW on their home ground. Which is exactly what Frankfurt Jaguar distributor Peter Lindner proceeded to do from 1961 with co-driver Peter Nöcker, first using an "old" 3.4 and then, in opalescent dark green, 3.8 Mk 2s initially prepared at Browns Lane to a specification drawn up by senior engineer Claude Baily.

There followed a string of victories at a variety of European circuits, though Lindner particularly shone at the unique and testing 14-mile Nurburgring circuit, where the 1962 and 1963 12-hour touring car events fell to the British Jaguars. Then in 1963 came the first European Touring Car Championship, to be won by Lindner's co-driver Peter Nöcker, after which the partnership transferred most of their efforts to Lindner's very special lightweight 'E' type — in which the German driver, who did so much to enhance Jaguar's standing on the continent, was tragically killed in 1964.

The Mk 2 did equally well in the less-publicised, but only marginally less competitive, saloon car races in such places as New Zealand and Australia, where the 3.8 Mk 2's useful track life was extended well into the mid-sixties; New Zealanders Ray Archibald and Tony Shelly, in fact, secured the car's last major endurance race win — the 1966 Pukekohe six-hours. While in Australia, Bob Jane virtually became a legend in his own lifetime with his seemingly invincible white 3.8, defeating the might of Holman & Moody-tuned Ford Galaxies, Chevrolet Impalas, Mustangs and Holdens; with regulations which gave more scope for engine modifications, Jane's car was equipped with larger valves, triple Weber carburettors, and a bored-and-stroked block, reckoned to produce well over 300bhp towards the end of its competitive life in 1965. Perhaps strangely, North America produced few results of note for the Mk 2, though star driver Walt Hansgen did take the wheel of a 3.8 with success on occasions.

In Britain, the Mk 2 helped promote what many people regard as a golden era of saloon car racing; many of the top Grand Prix drivers would take the wheel, usually for the two top teams of the day — Coombs, and Tommy Sopwith's *Equipe Endeavour.* Stirling Moss, Graham Hill, Roy Salvadori, Ivor Bueb, Bruce McLaren, Mike Parkes and Jack Sears were just a few of the "names" who, using Jaguar Mk 2s, dominated saloon car racing and delighted spectators all round the country during the early 'sixties. That is until the Impala and Galaxie entrants at last managed to obtain handling — and wheels! — that kept pace with the power produced by their massive V8s. The end for the 3.8 came around 1963 in Britain, hastened too by the lighter, and better handling, Ford Lotus Cortinas which heralded a new breed of sporting saloon.

The rally world saw the Mk 2 Jaguar garner great success, and the name of Bernard Consten is inseparable from the marque, thanks to a magnificent history of victories in the arduous Tour de France — four to be exact, the last being in 1963 against Ford Galaxie, Lotus Cortina and Alfa Romeo opposition. "Rally" is perhaps a too-simple description of this event, which mixed-in various racing circuits besides Alpine hillclimbs and other road stages across France. In true rallies, the Mk 2 does not in fact figure very extensively as, about the time the car appeared, international rallies were increasingly composed of "off-road" special stages where the Mk 2's weight and bulk worked against it. Thus the Mk 2 was never able to emulate the extensive successes of previous Jaguars in this sport, the 3.4 and MkVII saloons from different eras.

EVOLUTION

Production modifications

Note: dates and chassis/engine number change points are, in some cases, approximate as the factory sometimes incorporated modifications before, or after, the "official" change point.

You will find several of the car's serial numbers, collectively, stamped on a plate attached to bulkhead under the bonnet. The *chassis number* is also stamped on the bonnet catch channel forward of radiator, and on top of nearside frame member above the rear engine mounting bracket. The *engine number* is stamped on right-hand side of cylinder block above the oil filter, and at the front of the cylinder head casting. The *gearbox number* is stamped on a shoulder at the left-hand rear corner of the gearbox casing, and on the top cover.

Chassis numbers start at 100001 (RHD)/125001 (LHD) for 2.4-litre cars, 150001 (RHD)/ 175001 (LHD) for 3.4-litre cars, and 200001 (RHD)/210001 (LHD) for 3.8-litre cars. The suffix "DN" indicates that overdrive is fitted, "BW" automatic transmission and "P" power steering.

Engine numbers are prefixed "BG"-"BJ" (2.4-litre), "KG"-"KJ"

(3.4-litre) and "LA"-"LE" (3.8-litre). Suffixes "/7", "/8" and "/9" indicate compression ratio.

Gearbox number prefix letters indicate that overdrive is fitted.

October 1959: Jaguar Mk 2 introduced at the London Motor Show.

January 1960: Crankshaft rear cover assembly modified to improve sump sealing. BG.1317. KG.1327. LA.1500.

March 1960: 60lbs instead 100lbs oil pressure gauge fitted. 2.4, 101446/126370. 3.4, 151003/ 175499. 3.8, 200668/211867.

April 1960: Modified, telescopic, interior mirror fitted.

May 1960: Stiffer dampers fitted to front suspension. Paper filter replaces oil bath filter (3.4 and 3.8 cars only), previously optional. Oil bath filter now optional.

June 1960: Controls on upper steering column re-handed — standard transmission, flasher/ indicator stalk now on left, overdrive transmission, as above plus o/drive stalk to right. 2.4, 102242/125520. 3.4, 151466/ 175683. 3.8, 201087/212640.

July 1960: Water valve fitted to heater unit, coupled to temp. control flap in unit and operated by "Hot-Cold" control in car. 2.4, 102348/125529. 3.4, 151568/ 175697. 3.8, 201445/212774. Breather pipe added to petrol filler neck and non-vented cap fitted, to overcome petrol fumes.

September 1960: 5-inch pressed-steel wheels replace those with 4½-inch rims.

November 1960: Polythene brake fluid container replaces steel version. 2.4, 103503/125693. 3.4, 152171/175983. 3.8, 201702/ 213825. Swivelling type sun-visor replaces recessed type: 2.4, 103555/125696. 3.4, 152208/ 175989. 3.8, 201733/213857. Organ type accelerator pedal replaces pendant type (NB: first 165 RHD 46 LHD 3.4 and 4 RHD, 394 LHD 3.8 cars had organ-type). 3.4, 152275/176003. 3.8, 200005/ 213937. Door light frames modified to increase strength at waistline

(also affects door cappings). 2.4, 103850/125736. 3.4, 152398/ 176062. 3.8, 201870/214714. Modified oil filter assembly, downward inclined and with no drain plug, fitted. BG.5891. KG.4675. LA.7450. Boss in cylinder block for accepting electric engine heater transferred from left to right-hand side of block to avoid obstruction from exhaust pipes. KG.4104. LA.7214.

February 1961: Forged upper wishbones replace pressed type (interchangeable in sets). 2.4 pressed wheels, 104864/125898. 2.4 wire wheels, 104946/125903. 3.4 pressed wheels, 152964/ 176309. 3.4 wire wheels, 152983/ 176314. 3.8 pressed wheels, 202372/215151. 3.8 wire wheels, 202401/215155. Stiffer anti-roll bar (previously special order; requires new support brackets). 2.4, 105917/126131. 3.4, 153794/ 176668. 3.8, 203112/215816. Power steering conversion kit introduced for retrospective conversion of 3.4 and 3.8 cars, at £90.0.0d. Tube fitted to dipstick hole to assist replacement of dipstick, plus new dipstick with greater length between stop and bottom end. KG.5366. LA.8593.

June 1961: Rubber buffers fitted to outer rear corners of front and rear door sills to eliminate movement of doors when shut. "Zone" windscreen glass introduced.

August 1961: Front hub bearing water deflector incorporated (some cars fitted prior). 2.4 pressed wheels, 108734/126459. 2.4 wire wheels, 108872/126473. 3.4 pressed wheels, 155971/177302. 3.4 wire wheels, 156140/177342. 3.8 pressed wheels, 205346/ 217576. 3.8 wire wheels, 205519/ 217653. Roller type pump replaces eccentric rotor type on power assisted steering cars. KG.7700/ LB2634. Self-adjusting handbrake fitted (kits to convert earlier cars made available Dec.1961). 2.4, 108998/126479. 3.4, 156343/ 177360. 3.8, 205633/217696. Oil pump with longer body fitted, together with new sump with depression at front end. BG.9503. KG.7488. LB.2402. Engine breather coupled to air intake elbow connected to carburettors. BH.1166. KG.8272. LB.3922. Short-body SU fuel pump fitted.

October 1961: Cast iron instead of alloy crankshaft pulley fitted. BH.3894. KG.1349. LB.6271. Automatic fanbelt tensioner using spring-loaded jockey wheel fitted to power steering cars. KH.2146. LB.7222. On manual steering cars from. KH.3116. LB.8868.

December 1961: Modified crankshaft rear oil seal incorporating asbestos rope in an annular groove introduced; requires new rear end cover and crankshaft; BH.4551. KH.2794. LB.8247. Larger diameter prop. shaft universal joint fitted.

January 1962: Dipstick for auto trans moved from under centre console to engine bay. New type of exhaust manifold flange gasket with steel shell introduced, in conjunction with modified exhaust manifolds and downpipe. 3.4, 158296/177750. 3.8, 207228/ 219614. Seatbelt attachment points fitted. 2.4, 111418/126652. 3.4, 158371/177753. 3.8, 207313/ 219801. Waso combined ignition and steering lock fitted to all cars for Germany (optional on others at £7).

February 1962: Lucas C48 higher output dynamo made optional.

May 1962: Drilled camshafts fitted for quieter cold start. KH.4632. LC.2056. **September 1962:** Sealed beam headlight units replace bulb (flat) type for home market. 2.4, 112995. 3.4, 160201. 3.8, 208535.

October 1962: Longer main bearing cap dowels fitted on left-hand side of block (block machined to suit). BH.7969. KH.6481. LC.3827.

November 1962: 5-bolt instead of 4-bolt oil filter fitted. BH.7969. KH.7063. LC.4265.

January 1963: Reinforcement bracket fitted to Panhard rod body mounting. Gas-cell dampers fitted to reduce fade. 2.4, 114349/ 127012. 3.4, 161805/178844. 3.8, 209725/222048.

September 1963. Sealed for life propellor shaft fitted on automatic cars. 2.4, 115928/127270. 3.4, 164106/179468. 3.8, 231251/ 223042. Falling-flow (MkX type) power steering pump fitted to 3.4 and 3.8 cars. KJ.1497/LC.7303.

October 1963: Centre horn button now live in addition to horn ring. 2.4, 116114/127312. 3.4, 164402/ 179499. 3.8, 231586/223125.

January 1964: Cast aluminium sump fitted with revised oil pipes and pump (packing pieces under anti-roll bar required). 2.4, BJ.2264 3.4, KJ.2791. 3.8, LC.8068.

March 1964: Modified pistons with chamfer and drain holes below oil control ring to improve oil consumption (3.8 only). LC.8895. Grease nipples fitted to front hubs on pressed-wheel cars; improved grease seals fitted to tie-rod ball joints and wheel swivels with bleed hole covered by nylon washer. 2.4, 116730/127486. 3.4, 166075/179733. 3.8, 232331/ 223447.

May 1964: Type AUF 301 fuel pump fitted (as for S-type). Steering idler assembly with taper roller bearings fitted. 2.4, 117585/ 127544. 3.4, 166588/179841. 3.8, 232641/223644.

October 1964: Brake disc shields fitted to reduce tendency of inner pads to wear more quickly than outer. 2.4, 118052/127636. 3.4, 167631/179994. 3.8, 233264/ 223960.

June 1965: Type 35 (PRN.D1. D2.L) automatic transmission

replaces DG (PNDLR). 3.4, 171615/181429. 3.8, 235332/ 224738. Waterproof cover for distributor introduced.

September 1965: All-synchro gearbox fitted. 2.4, 119200/ 127822. 3.4, 169341/180188. 3.8, 234125/224150. Diaphragm clutch fitted. KJ.8237. LE.2981.

April 1966: Switch incorporated in heated rear window circuit. 2.4, 119902/127998. 3.4, 170565/ 180398. 3.8, 235046/224417. Lucas 9H horns replace 618U type. Direction indicator switch improved.

May 1966: Lucas 5SJ windscreen washer (with plastic reservoir) replaces glass type.

July 1967: Dunlop brakes replaced by Girling. 2.4, 121150/128156. 3.4, 171380/180814. 3.8, 235263/ 224654. Improved boot lock with revised cam fitted, to prevent lid from opening on road. 2.4, 121267/128280. 3.4, 171582/ 181311. 3.8, 235304/224706. Varamatic steering introduced on (RHD) 3.4 and 3.8 cars. 3.4, 171583. 3.8, 235312.
New wire-wheels with forged hubs and straight spokes fitted. 2.4, 121316/128321. 3.4, 171638/181429. 3.8, 235309/ 224714.

September 1967: Mk 2 superseded by the "240" and "340" model Jaguars.

SPECIFICATION

Jaguar Mk2 2.4-litre Saloon

Type designation	Jaguar Mark 2, 2.4-litre saloon.
Built	Allesley, Coventry, 1959-1967.
Numbers made	3,405 left-hand-drive, 22,768 right-hand-drive.
Drive configuration	Front engine, rear-wheel-drive.

Engine
Type: Cast iron block, six-cylinders in-line, overhead camshafts working in aluminium alloy, hemispherical combustion chamber cylinder head.
Camshafts: Overhead; one inlet, one exhaust.
Capacity: 2483cc (151.5cu.in).
Compression ratio: 8:1 (7 or 9:1 optional).
Bore & stroke: 83x76.5mm (3.268x3.01in).
Maximum power: 120bhp @ 5,750rpm (gross).
Maximum torque: 144ft.lbs. @ 2,000rpm (gross).
Carburettors: Two 24mm Solex.

Transmission (manual) — Four-speed single helical gearbox with synchromesh on 2nd, 3rd and top, mounted in-line with engine and driving through single dry plate 10 in. diameter clutch. Optional Laycock de Normanville overdrive.

Transmission (automatic) — Borg Warner DG or Type 35 three-speed.
Ratios (standard): 1st and reverse 14.42:1 (15.36), 2nd 7.94 (8.46), 3rd 5.48 (5.84), top 4.27 (4.55).
Figures in brackets are for overdrive car — overdrive top is 3.54.
Automatic: Low 21.2-9.86, Intermediate 13.2-6.14, top 4.27.

Final drive — Hypoid, semi-floating, in Salisbury 4HA live rear axle.
Ratios: 4.27 (standard and automatic), 4.55 (overdrive). Other ratios available to special order including 4.09, 4.55, 3.27, 2.93 etc.

Wheelbase — 8ft. 11.38in.

Track	Pressed wheels: 4ft. 7in. front, 4ft. 5.38in. rear. Wire-wheels: 4ft. 7.5in. front, 4ft. 6.3in. rear.
Suspension	Front: independent, subframe mounted with semi-trailing double wishbones, coil springs, telescopic dampers and anti-roll bar. Rear: trailing link by cantilever semi-elliptic springs, incorporating twin parallel radius arms, Panhard rod and telescopic dampers.
Steering	Burman recirculating ball and 17in. adjustable two-spoke steering wheel, 4.8 turns lock-to-lock (3.5 turns optional high ratio box); power steering with Hobourn Eaton pump optional, also 4.8 turns lock-to-lock. Turning circle 33 ½ ft.
Brakes	Dunlop disc with vacuum servo assistance; square quick-change pads. 11in. discs front, 11.375in. rear.
Wheels & Tyres	Pressed steel bolt-on 15in. diameter 4.5K (later 5K), wire wheel 15in. diameter 5K, knock-off optional. Dunlop 6.40x15 Road Speed tyres.
Bodywork	Jaguar-designed, unitary all-steel construction with main components by the Pressed Steel Company, Oxford. Sole body type — four-door five-seat saloon. Dimensions: length 15ft. 0.75in., width 5ft. 6.75in., height 4ft. 9.75in.
Weight	28.5cwt distributed 56% front/44% rear (approx.)
Electrical system	Lucas 12-volt by dynamo and single battery, positive earth. Lucas distributor type DMBZ6. Lighting: Lucas F700 60/36 watts home and RHD export; 45/40 continental, 45/36 France, sealed-beam units 60/36 for USA. Fog lamp: Lucas type 5WFT. Driving lamp: Lucas type 490.
Performance	(from *Autocar's* "Used Car" test as no contemporary data available) Overdrive: Max. speed 96.3mph. Acceleration 0-60mph 17.3 secs; standing ¼-mile 20.8 secs. Fuel consumption 18mpg.

Jaguar Mk2 3.4-litre Saloon

Type designation	Jaguar Mark 2, 3.4-litre saloon.
Built	Allesley, Coventry, 1959-1967.
Numbers made	6,571 left-hand-drive, 22,095 right-hand-drive.
Drive configuration	Front engine, rear-wheel-drive.
Engine Type: Camshafts: Capacity: Compression ratio: Bore & stroke:	 Cast iron block, six-cylinders in-line, overhead camshafts working in aluminium alloy, hemispherical combustion chamber cylinder head. Overhead; one inlet, one exhaust. 3442cc (209.96cu.in). 8:1 (7 or 9:1 optional). 83x106mm (3.268x4.173in).

Maximum power:	210bhp @ 5,500rpm (gross).
Maximum torque:	215ft.lbs. @ 3,000rpm (gross).
Carburettors:	Two 1¾in. HD6 SU.

Transmission (manual)
Four-speed single helical gearbox with synchromesh on 2nd, 3rd and top, mounted in-line with engine and driving through single dry plate 10 in. diameter clutch. Optional Laycock de Normanville overdrive.
Ratios (standard): 1st and reverse 11.95:1 (10.55), 2nd 6.584 (6.20), 3rd 4.541 (4.28), top 3.54 (3.54).
Overdrive: 1st and reverse 12.73:1 (11.28), 2nd 7.012 (6.597), 3rd 4.836 (4.561), direct top 3.77 (3.77), overdrive 2.933 (2.933). Figures in brackets are for close ratio gears.

Transmission (automatic)
Borg Warner DG or Type 35 three-speed.
Ratios: Low 17.6 — 8.16, Intermediate 10.95 - 5.08, top 3.54.

Final drive
Hypoid, semi-floating, in Salisbury 4HA live rear axle. Thornton Powr-Lok limited slip device standard on 3.8, optional on 3.4.
Ratios: 3.54 (standard and automatic), 3.77 (overdrive). Other ratios available to special order including 4.09, 4.55, 3.27, 2.93 etc.

Wheelbase
8ft. 11.38in.

Track
Pressed steel wheels: 4ft. 7in. front, 4ft. 5.38in. rear. Wire-wheels: 4ft. 7.5in. front, 4ft. 6.3in. rear.

Suspension
Front: independent, subframe mounted with semi-trailing double wishbones, coil springs, telescopic dampers and anti-roll bar.
Rear: trailing link by cantilever semi-elliptic springs, incorporating twin parallel radius arms, Panhard rod and telescopic dampers.

Steering
Burman recirculating ball and 17in. adjustable two-spoke steering wheel; 4.8 turns lock-to-lock (3.5 turns optional high ratio box); power steering with Hobourn Eaton pump optional, also 4.8 turns lock-to-lock. Turning circle 33½ft.

Brakes
Dunlop (later Girling) disc with vacuum servo assistance; square quick-change pads. 11in. discs front, 11.375in. rear.

Wheels & Tyres
Pressed steel bolt-on 15in. diameter 4.5K (later 5K), wire wheel 15ins. diameter 5K, knock-off, optional. Dunlop 6.40x15 Road Speed tyres.

Bodywork
Jaguar-designed, unitary all-steel construction with main components by the Pressed Steel Company, Oxford. Sole body type — four-door five-seat saloon.
Dimensions: length 15ft. 0.75in., width 5ft. 6.75in., height 4ft. 9.75in.

Weight
29.5cwt distributed 59% front/41% rear (approx.)

Electrical system
Lucas 12-volt by dynamo and single battery, positive earth. Lucas distributor type DMBZ6.
Lighting: Lucas F700 60/36 watts home and RHD export; 45/40 continental, 45/36 France, sealed-beam units 60/36 for USA. Fog lamp: Lucas type 5WFT. Driving lamp: Lucas type 490.

**Performance
(manual with overdrive)**
Max. speed 120mph. Speeds in gears: 1st 35mph, 2nd 64mph, 3rd 97mph, direct top 119mph. Acceleration 0-60mph 10.5 secs (estimated); standing ¼-mile 17.2 secs (estimated). Fuel consumption 17mpg.

Performance (automatic)	Max. speed 119.9mph. Speeds in gears: low 51mph, intermediate 82mph. Acceleration 0-60mph 11.9 secs; standing ¼-mile 19.1 secs. Fuel consumption 16mpg.

Jaguar Mk2 3.8-litre Saloon

Type designation	Jaguar Mark 2, 3.8-litre saloon.
Built	Allesley, Coventry, 1959-1967.
Numbers made	14,758 left-hand-drive; 15,383 right-hand-drive.
Drive configuration	Front engine, rear-wheel-drive.
Engine Type: Camshafts: Capacity: Compression ratio: Bore & stroke: Maximum power: Maximum torque: Carburettors:	 Cast iron block, six-cylinders in-line, overhead camshafts working in aluminium alloy, hemispherical combustion chamber cylinder-head. Overhead, one inlet, one exhaust. 3781cc (230.65cu.in). 8:1 (7 or 9:1 optional). 87x106mm (3.425 x 4.173in). 220bhp @ 5,500rpm (gross). 240ft.lbs. @ 3,000 rpm (gross). Two 1¾in. HD6 SU.
Transmission (manual)	Four-speed single helical gearbox with synchromesh on 2nd, 3rd and top, mounted in-line with engine and driving through single dry plate 10in. diameter clutch. Optional Laycock de Normanville overdrive. Ratios (standard): 1st and reverse 11.95:1 (10.55), 2nd 6.584 (6.20), 3rd 4.541 (4.28), top 3.54 (3.54). Overdrive: 1st and reverse 12.73:1 (11.28), 2nd 7.012 (6.597), 3rd 4.836 (4.561), direct top 3.77 (3.77), overdrive 2.933 (2.933). Figures in brackets are for close ratio gears.
Transmission (automatic)	Borg Warner DG or Type 35 three-speed. Ratios: Low 17.6-8.16, Intermediate 10.95-5.08, top 3.54.
Final drive	Hypoid, semi-floating, in Salisbury 4HA live rear axle. Thornton Powr-Lok limited slip device standard on 3.8, optional on 3.4. Ratios: 3.54 (standard and automatic), 3.77 (overdrive). Other ratios available to special order including 4.09, 4.55, 3.27, 2.93 etc.
Wheelbase	8ft. 11.38in.
Track	Pressed steel wheels: 4ft. 7in. front, 4ft. 5.38in. rear. Wire-wheels: 4ft. 7.5in. front, 4ft. 6.3in. rear.
Suspension	Front: independent, subframe mounted with semi-trailing double wishbones, coil springs, telescopic dampers and anti-roll bar. Rear: trailing link by cantilever semi-elliptic springs, incorporating twin parallel radius arms, Panhard rod and telescopic dampers.
Steering	Burman recirculating ball and 17in. adjustable two-spoke steering wheel; 4.8 turns lock-to-lock (3.5 turns optional high ratio box); power steering with Hobourn Eaton pump optional, also 4.8 turns lock-to-lock. Turning circle 33½ft.

Brakes	Dunlop disc with vacuum servo assistance; square quick-change pads. 11in. discs front, 11.375in. rear.
Wheels & tyres	Pressed steel bolt-on 15in. diameter 4.5K (later 5K), wire-wheel 15in. diameter 5K, knock-off, optional. Dunlop 6.40x15 Road Speed tyres.
Bodywork	Jaguar-designed, unitary all-steel construction with main components by the Pressed Steel Company, Oxford. Sole body type — four-door five-seat saloon. Dimensions: length 15ft. 0.75in., width 5ft. 6.75in., height 4ft. 9.75in.
Weight	30cwt distributed 59% front/41% rear approx.
Electrical system	Lucas 12 volt by dynamo and single battery, positive earth. Lucas distributor type DMBZ6. Lighting: Lucas F700 60/36 watts home and RHD export; 45/40 continental, 45/36 France, sealed-beam units 60/36 for USA. Foglamp: Lucas type 5WFT. Driving lamp: Lucas type 490.
Performance (manual with overdrive)	Max. speed 125mph. Speeds in gears: 1st 35mph, 2nd 64mph, 3rd 98mph, direct top 120mph. Acceleration 0-60mph 8.5 secs; standing ¼-mile 16.3 secs. Fuel consumption 15.7mpg.
Performance (automatic)	Max. speed 120.4mph. Speeds in gears: low 50mph, intermediate 81mph. Acceleration 0-60mph 9.8 secs; standing ¼-mile 17.2 secs. Fuel consumption 17.3mpg.

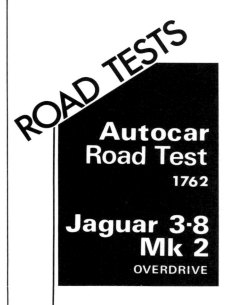

ROAD TESTS

Autocar Road Test 1762

Jaguar 3·8 Mk 2
OVERDRIVE

Always a good looker, the Jaguar in Mk. 2 style with larger windows and slim pillars, is a much improved car

VERY few cars indeed set out to offer so much as the 3.8-litre Mk. 2 Jaguar, and none can match it in terms of value for money. In one compact car an owner has *Gran Turismo* performance, town carriage manners and luxurious family appointments.

The model in its latest Mk. 2 version as tested is the outcome of several years of development, since it was first introduced (with 2.4-litre engine) in September 1955. The changes made for 1960* without doubt represent together the greatest improvement so far achieved between a Jaguar model and its predecessor—short of a wholly new design.

Externally, the rather wider (by 3½in) rear track is quickly noticed; it is not a very significant design change but it plays its part, with other minor improvements, in providing a more stable ride with increased resistance to roll when cornering. The 3.8-litre engine, which has an 87mm stroke compared with 83mm for the 3.4-litre unit, has lost none of its sweetness nor flexibility in producing an extra 10 b.h.p., and 240 lb ft torque instead of 215—at 3,000 r.p.m. What is more, this big twin-cam engine apparently has no objection to revving momentarily to its extreme limit of 6,000 r.p.m. This figure was touched or approached on several occasions during the test without the engine losing tune or showing any sign of distress. The normal limit—and there is little advantage in exceeding it—is 5,500 r.p.m.

When one examines the appearance and interior arrangements, marked improvements are apparent at once. The larger windows and screen, with slim chromium frames, brighten the car both inside and out. A new and much superior instrument layout has been introduced for the driver, and a central leather-trimmed console carrying the radio installation and heater control quadrants now merges with the transmission hump, and has a large covered ashtray buried in it. The steering wheel, too, is of pleasing new design, having two safety-flat spokes beneath a horn half-ring, and a rim that is comfortable to grasp. Matched tumbler switches are identified on a transparent strip beneath them, which has internal-glow illumination at night.

No one will have doubted that the performance of this 3.8 saloon would prove exceptional; a standing quarter-mile in under 16.5 seconds is matched by a 0-100 m.p.h. figure of 25.1 seconds and a maximum of 125 m.p.h. At the other end of the scale this four- occasional five-seater saloon will also glide silently in heavy traffic, snatch-free in top gear, down to 14 m.p.h. But the aspects of the performance which our drivers most appreciated were the smooth, silent cruising up to 100 m.p.h. in overdrive top on auto-routes at home and on the Continent, and the splendid acceleration for quick, safe overtaking, in direct top or third.

It is proper to turn attention directly from speed to brakes. The Dunlop 12in discs, as the recorded data indicate, are very powerful indeed. The pedal pressures, up to a maximum of 95 lb, are well matched against retardation

*The Mk. 2 improvements were described in detail in *The Autocar* of 2 October, 1959, p. 289-291.

which itself reaches almost the theoretical maximum. Repeated use of the brakes from high speeds caused no loss of stopping power, unevenness or increase in pedal pressures. The front brakes did feel "cobbley" when they became exceptionally hot, but recovered as they cooled.

The hand brake, a good big lever on the outside of the driver's seat, is satisfactory for all ordinary uses, though like most disc systems of its kind, it will not hold the car on a 1-in-4 test gradient. A red "on" warning light is provided which also signals if the brake fluid level is low. The brakes may be summed up by saying that they proved completely dependable throughout the test.

The car tested has a Laycock de Normanville overdrive, for top gear only, giving 26.4 m.p.h. per 1,000 r.p.m. in conjunction with a 3.77 to 1 axle ratio. The overdrive switch—a short lever mounted on the left side of the steering column, needs heavier spring loading on the test car; the brush of a sleeve will move it. Such is the power available that overdrive serves as a high top for nearly all out-of-town driving, and progress is the more silent and restful as a result.

Maximum speed is attained in overdrive, normal peak revs being reached in direct top at about 115 m.p.h. For smooth engagement of direct top from overdrive, plenty of throttle is desirable, and from top to overdrive, also some throttle.

No changes have been made in the familiar Jaguar gear box; the intermediate ratios are well chosen, and quiet in use. Leisurely changes can be made very sweetly, but the synchromesh is weak and the lever movements are rather long; when the box became hot the lever movement between bottom and second was stiff.

In the course of performance measurements a clutch naturally comes in for some heavy treatment; that on the 3.8 was very good indeed. Never was there any slip or roughness in engagement in spite of the very considerable torque transmitted. The pedal load is not unduly heavy, but a shorter travel would be appreciated.

Overall fuel consumption, including extensive performance testing at the Motor Industry Research Association track and on the Continent, was 15.7 m.p.g. for 1,690 miles. A brisk run of 221 miles in England returned exactly 17 m.p.g.; another of 349 miles, on both sides of the Channel, 18.9 m.p.g. A spell of gentle driving on British roads gave 21 m.p.g. The load was mainly two passengers and some luggage, but a full load was carried at times. Ordinary premium fuel was used without any signs of pinking. In France and Belgium the best available fuel suited the car well enough. Accommodation of the fuel tank has been something of a problem. Holding just over 12 gallons, it is smaller than that of the original 2.4 model. Total oil consumption during the test was 4.5 pints.

Suspensions seldom have to be designed for such a wide variety of speeds and conditions as that provided by the 3.8 Jaguar. Few owners will be other than well satisfied, for

Tastefully trimmed and upholstered in hide and with polished veneers, the 3.8 interior has also a full complement of equipment and comforts. There are arm rests and pockets on all doors

there is sufficient firmness for fast driving, yet the ride is smooth and comfortable over all but the worst road surfaces. The pitching which a hump or ridge will induce is damped at once, and rolling movements are firmly restrained. From a following car, the suspension may be observed absorbing road irregularities with a whole variety of movements not transmitted to the passengers.

An important improvement in the Mk. 2 is the complete elimination of the rear axle hop or tramping which handicapped some earlier models when using full acceleration from a standstill. This may be largely the result of the fitting, as a standard feature, of a Powr-Lok limited-slip differential. For optimum get-away from a standstill, between 1,500 and 2,000 r.p.m. seemed best for clutch engagement.

Very little wheel noise or thump can be sensed in the car, and no reaction is felt at the steering wheel (the column of which now includes three universal joints). Over rough roads a slight body shake was noted at the front door pillars. With the windows closed, the interior silence is remarkable, particularly when overdrive is in use; an occasional moaning may be heard from the back axle.

As a result of careful design the quarter-lights may be opened even at high speed without causing more than very slight wind roar. They are spring-loaded on the test car to stay at about a 40 deg angle, which is the most silent and draught-free position, and there are also 90 deg and 130 deg positions. The exhaust note is very restrained, being scarcely audible inside the car.

There are three recommended pairs of tyre pressures, of which the normal is 25 lb sq in (1.76 kg sq cm) front and 22 lb sq in (1.55 kg sq cm) back. During the test the opinion was formed that the car handled better for general driving with an all-round increase of 3–4 lb sq in cold; this makes very little difference to the ride comfort. For fast cruising a 31/28 setting is recommended by the manufacturers, and maximum speed figures were obtained at 34/31—also according to the handbook. The handling of the car does not seem to be affected appreciably by the extent of the load carried, within normal limits.

Pronounced understeer is a characteristic of this Jaguar— the wide slip angle on the front tyres is clearly seen by an observer. The steering is better suited to the low and moderate speed sections of the car's wide range. Rather than comment upon what is a quite well-known design, it may be more helpful to discuss the feel and functioning. For manœuvring and parking the steering is rather heavy, and sufficiently low geared to require a fair amount of wheel-winding. Ordinary guidance in a traffic stream requires only light and gentle movements, while with more lock for sharp bends the heaviness increases. As speeds rise over about 50 m.p.h. there is increasing need to take bends early and to hold the car tight into them, otherwise it may swing wider than intended. There is quite powerful self-centring and this, no doubt, is in part responsible for the good line that the car holds on straight roads at all speeds. Up to about 100 m.p.h. side winds have little effect on the car; above this speed (and strong side winds were experienced at times during the testing) quick and delicate corrections were needed to hold course.

Since there is sufficient power to spin the rear wheels quite readily in third gear on wet roads, and because the weight distribution is markedly in favour of the front, care has to be taken to use only light throttle when coming out of bends or away from corners; experienced drivers likely to be attracted by the 3.8 will adopt this technique instinctively. Incidentally, the stiff and notchy accelerator linkage of some earlier models has been redesigned; it is now smooth, light and progressive in its action.

Should the back end of the car slide, lifting the accelerator foot is usually enough to check it at once. Here, however, the low-geared steering—5 turns lock to lock with rather slow response around the mid-sector—is at a disadvantage, and it is difficult to apply quickly enough opposite helm to correct a skid at once. Worn tyres can have the effect of slowing the steering response. The turning circle between kerbs of just under 36ft is good in relation to the car's dimensions. On certain dry road surfaces there is some tyre squeal, but it is seldom at all obtrusive.

This Jaguar is one of the comparatively few cars in which any size of driver should be able to make himself comfortable. The seat has a long slide, the rails rising gently to their front ends, and the steering column has a convenient rake and a long adjustment. Obviously great care has been taken with the arrangement of hand controls and instruments. The pedals are not quite up to this high

Left: the neat, smart and convenient new panel arrangement and steering wheel. Right: a large and handsome engine in a small space. Most components likely to need routine attention have been raised to accessible positions

Jaguar 3.8 Mk. 2 . . .

Wide-track rear wheels and full-width window characterize the latest Jaguar model from this view, taken at Boom while the car was being tested in Belgium

standard, for there is a discrepancy in the levels of accelerator and brake pedals, and it is scarcely possible to heel/toe, though frequently desirable to do so. Certain drivers found the accelerator pedal (no longer of the organ type) and its angle of movement a little inconvenient.

Increased screen and window area have, of course, improved all-round vision. The scuttle no longer seems high, and the steering wheel rim is below the immediate horizon of bonnet top and front wings. Since the screen pillars and the sealing strips for the glass are thin, there is very little blind area. A wide new rear-view mirror, top mounted, takes advantage of the full-width rear window, and does not interrupt the forward view. Two sun vizors are neatly flush-fitted into the roof. They are effective, but when extended remain rather too close to the forehead.

In wet weather, vision is less good since the area swept by the driver's wiper blade is too small and stops well short of the bottom rail. The linkage produces a clicking noise. A toughened glass screen is normally fitted to cars delivered in the home market; owners may specify a laminated screen at an extra cost of £7 8s 6d inclusive of P.T.

At night, maximum speed must obviously be restricted, but the head lamps are powerful. As delivered, the setting was rather too low for maximum range with the result that cut-off, when dipped, was to the close, foreign standard. A head lamp semaphore switch is provided, operated by lifting the turn indicator lever on the steering column.

It is unusual these days to find side lamps which are fitted as separate units faired into the tops of the front wings, but there is much to be said for this arrangement. On the Mark 2 Jaguars the lamps are tiny and carry red "tell-tales" in their tops. A tall driver can just see the top of the near-side lamp from his seat.

Jaguars fit a pair of bright, semi-built-in auxiliary lamps. These are particularly good for winding secondary roads but seem rather too strong for straight main roads, since oncoming drivers regularly show disapproval. No fog was encountered to test them in those conditions. A bright reversing lamp is switched on with the engagement of reverse gear.

The excellent new instrument and control layout has already been mentioned. Among the supra-mundane

Auxiliary lamps are now flush-fitted in front of the horn grilles, so tidying up the frontal appearance. Diminutive side lamps are neatly faired into the wing brows; they have "tell-tales" on top

equipment are the cigarette lighter and handsome covered ashtray (two more neat, covered ashtrays are let into the rear arm rests); small polished veneer tables folding from the backs of the front seats; rear-seat heating duct; a map light and a separate blue light in the dash locker; a large tachometer paired with the speedometer; smaller matching dials for water temperature, oil pressure and ammeter in addition to the fuel gauge. Their illumination at night is clear and subdued, and no reflections were seen in the screen. There is no positive fuel reserve, but an amber lamp warns of the need to refill. The horns have a penetrating, high-frequency note.

Extensive use is made of hide leather and fine veneer in the interior trimming. The floor is carpeted, and reinforced under the driver's heels. The roof is cloth-trimmed, to meet customers' demand and Jaguar standards of silence, we learn. Large and comfortable seats are fitted; at the back there is a central folding arm rest. The front pair with advantage might have a little more curvature to give greater cornering location to the occupants.

If the front seats are set in their rearmost positions, knee-room for the back passengers is restricted. It is very easy to get in or out of all the doors, and sill height is such that, although the car is quite low-built, they do not catch a high kerb. The doors carry pockets and arm rests, and courtesy lamps are lit when a door is opened. The courtesy-cum-interior lamps are not, perhaps, in the best position—beside the rear passengers at the points where they might wish to rest their heads.

The test car is fitted with an H.M.V. radio, neatly built in, together with its speaker, below the instrument panel. The tone was good and there was no distortion at high volume. The aerial mounted on the offside front wing can be retracted or extended with the aid of a winder mounted horizontally under the instrument panel on the driver's side.

A comprehensive heating and ventilation system is neatly built in. A scuttle ventilator may be opened to admit fresh air, with the aid of a lever inside the map-slot beneath the switch line-up. Selector levers, flanking the radio, give varying degrees of heat and rate of delivery to screen or car interior, or both. A two-speed fan is provided which operates very quietly. The central air duct to the rear seats has already been mentioned. Since the engine is controlled to run at about 90 deg C, a greater heat supply might be expected; it was just sufficient on the test car for comfort when the outside temperature was at freezing point. The car interior is well sealed against draughts and fumes, and no water entered it in torrential rain.

Much luggage can be stowed in the boot. Should it be necessary to change a wheel, jack and handle are found in clips in the boot, and the spare is beneath the carpet, in a hatch in the floor. The screwjack is a sturdy, triangulated affair, with a lifting bar to slide into any one of four sockets. The quite elaborate tool kit is carried in rubber in a circular box which fits snugly into the well of the spare wheel. If the car jack is used to change a rear wheel, the semi-spats need not be removed, since the wheel drops on the springs; but a garage jack, giving a central lift, leaves insufficient clearance. In any case only two quick-release screw fasteners need be undone to remove a spat.

Like the lid of the luggage boot, the bonnet lid, hinged at the rear, is spring loaded; a control in the car releases the first catch. The engine compartment is a sight for enthusiastic eyes, being tightly filled by the big, bright,

Jaguar 3.8 Mk. 2 . . .

twin-cam engine. Parts likely to need attention are fairly accessible and fillers are easily reached—oil, water, brake fluid, windscreen washer and enclosed battery (through the hinge gap of the open bonnet if one wishes). The oil dip stick is easily withdrawn, but difficult to replace; level readings should not be taken until the engine has been standing for some minutes, owing to the slow drain-down.

The Mark 2 3.8 Jaguar was introduced in October last year with a special eye on the American market, and with automatic transmission much in mind. Such a model is even better suited to American roads and journeys and offers even better value than its predecessors. The manual change model tested is a very distinguished car; it calls for an experienced driver to take full advantage of its great potential.

JAGUAR 3.8 MK. 2 OVERDRIVE SALOON

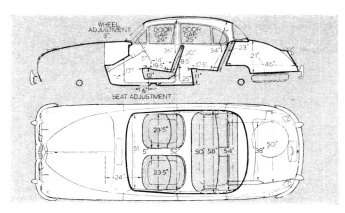

Scale ⅛in. to 1ft. Driving seat in central position. Cushions uncompressed.

——— DATA ———

PRICE (basic), with saloon body, £1,300. British purchase tax, £542 15s 10d. Total (in Great Britain), £1,842 15s 10d. Extras: H.M.V. radio £47 15s 2d.

ENGINE: Capacity, 3,781 c.c. (230.6 cu in)
Number of cylinders, 6.
Bore and stroke, 87 × 106mm (3.425 × 4.173in).
Valve gear, 2 overhead camshafts.
Compression ratio, 8 to 1.
B.h.p. 220 at 5,500 r.p.m. (B.h.p. per ton laden 133.7).
Torque, 240 lb ft at 3,000 r.p.m.
M.p.h. per 1,000 r.p.m. in top gear, 20.5; O.D. top 26.4.

WEIGHT: (With 5 gals fuel) 29.9 cwt (3,350 lb).
Weight distribution (per cent): F, 56.5; R, 43.5.
Laden as tested, 32.9 cwt (3,686 lb).
Lb per c.c. (laden), 0.97.

BRAKES: Type, Dunlop disc with quick-change pads.
Method of operation, hydraulic vacuum servo assisted.
Disc diameter: F, 11in; R, 11.375in.
Swept area: 495 sq in total (300 sq in per ton laden).

TYRES: 6.40—15in Dunlop Road Speed.
Pressures (lb sq in): F, 25; R, 22 (normal). F, 31; R, 28 (fast driving).

TANK CAPACITY: 12 Imperial gallons.
Oil sump, 13 pints.
Cooling system, 20 pints.

DIMENSIONS: Wheelbase, 8ft 11.375in.
Track; F, 4ft 7in; R, 4ft 5.375in.
Length (overall), 15ft 0.75in.
Width, 5ft 6.75in.
Height, 4ft 9.5in.
Ground clearance, 7in.
Capacity of luggage space: 13 cu ft (approx).

ELECTRICAL SYSTEM: 12-volt; 67 ampère-hour battery.
Head lights, Double dip; 60-36 watt bulbs.

SUSPENSION: Front, Independent, wishbones, coil springs, telescopic dampers, anti-roll bar.
Rear, Cantilever, half elliptic springs, radius arms, Panhard rod, telescopic dampers.

——— **PERFORMANCE** ———

ACCELERATION TIMES (mean):
Speed range, Gear Ratios and Time in Sec.:

M.P.H.	*2.933 to 1	3.77 to 1	4.836 to 1	7.012 to 1	12.731 to 1
10—30	—	6.7	5.1	3.1	2.5
20—40	—	6.0	4.7	3.4	—
30—50	8.5	6.1	4.9	3.6	—
40—60	7.8	5.7	4.2	—	—
50—70	8.6	5.9	4.9	—	—
60—80	9.3	6.3	5.3	—	—
70—90	9.5	7.7	6.5	—	—
80—100	12.7	9.7	—	—	—
90—110	19.2	15.5	—	—	—

*Overdrive

From rest through gears to:

30 m.p.h.	3.2 sec.	
40	,,	4.9 ,,
50	,,	6.4 ,,
60	,,	8.5 ,,
70	,,	11.7 ,,
80	,,	14.6 ,,
90	,,	18.2 ,,
100	,,	25.1 ,,
110	,,	33.2 ,,

Standing quarter mile 16.3 sec.

MAXIMUM SPEEDS ON GEARS:

Gear			M.p.h.	K.p.h.
O.D.	..	(mean)	125.0	201.2
		(best)	126.0	202.8
Top	..	..	120.0	193.1
3rd	..	..	98.0	157.7
2nd	..	..	64.0	103.0
1st	..	..	35.0	56.3

SPEEDOMETER: 2 m.p.h. fast from 30—120 m.p.h.

TRACTIVE EFFORT (by Tapley meter):

			Pull (lb per ton)	Equivalent gradient
O.D.	..	..	270	1 in 8.2
Top	..	..	365	1 in 6.0
Third	..	..	455	1 in 4.9
Second	..	..	610	1 in 3.6

BRAKES (at 30 m.p.h. in neutral):

Pedal load in lb.	Retardation	Equiv. stopping distance in ft.
25	0.30g	100
50	0.49g	61
75	0.80g	38
100	0.96g	31.4

FUEL CONSUMPTION (at steady speeds):

		Direct Top	O.D. Top
30 m.p.h.		27.7	31.7
40	,,	24.3	29.8
50	,,	23.5	27.7
60	,,	21.5	25.0
70	,,	20.4	23.2
80	,,	17.1	20.0
90	,,	14.9	17.5
100	,,	12.2	15.5

Overall fuel consumption for 1,690 miles, 15.7 m.p.g. (18.0 litres per 100 km.).
Approximate normal range 15—22 m.p.g. (18.8-12.8 litres per 100 km.).
Fuel: Premium grade.

TEST CONDITIONS: Weather: Dry, light wind—strong gusts.
Air temperature, 48 deg. F.

STEERING: Turning circle:
Between kerbs, L, 35ft 10in, R, 35ft 9in.
Between walls, L, 37ft 9in, R, 37ft 8in.
Turns of steering wheel from lock to lock, 5.

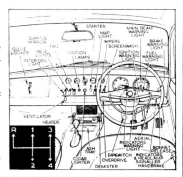

The Motor Road Test No. 29/61

Make: Jaguar   **Makers:** Jaguar Cars, Ltd., Coventry.

Type: 3.4 litre Mark 2 (automatic transmission and power steering)

Test Data

World copyright reserved: no unauthorized reproduction in whole or in part.

CONDITIONS: Weather: Mild and dry with light breeze. (Temperature 54°–58°F., Barometer 29.4 in. Hg.) Surface: Dry tarred macadam and concrete. Fuel: Premium-grade pump petrol (approx 97 Research Method Octane Rating).

INSTRUMENTS
Speedometer at 30 m.p.h.	..	1% fast
Speedometer at 60 m.p.h.	..	3% fast
Speedometer at 90 m.p.h.	..	3% fast
Speedometer at 120 m.p.h.	..	3% fast
Distance recorder	..	3", slow

WEIGHT
Kerb weight (unladen, but with oil coolant and fuel for approx. 50 miles) .. 30½ cwt.
Front/rear distribution of kerb weight.. 59/41
Weight laden as tested .. 34 cwt.

MAXIMUM SPEEDS
Flying Mile
Mean of six opposite runs .. 119.9 m.p.h.
Best one-way time equals .. 120.8 m.p.h.
"Maximile" Speed (Timed quarter mile after one mile accelerating from rest)
Mean of four opposite runs .. 113.4 m.p.h.
Best one-way time equals .. 115.4 m.p.h.
Speed in gears (automatic upward changes)
Max. speed in 2nd gear .. .. 73 m.p.h.
Max. speed in 1st gear .. .. 45 m.p.h.
Speed in gears (at 5,500 r.p.m. using manual "hold" controls)
Max. speed in 2nd gear .. .. 82 m.p.h.
Max. speed in 1st gear .. .. 51 m.p.h.

FUEL CONSUMPTION
26.5 m.p.g. at constant 30 m.p.h. on level
25.5 m.p.g. at constant 40 m.p.h. on level.
23.5 m.p.g. at constant 50 m.p.h. on level.
22.0 m.p.g. at constant 60 m.p.h. on level.
20.5 m.p.g. at constant 70 m.p.h. on level.
19.0 m.p.g. at constant 80 m.p.h. on level.
17.0 m.p.g. at constant 90 m.p.h. on level.
14.5 m.p.g. at constant 100 m.p.h. on level

Overall Fuel Consumption for 1,674 miles. 104.6 gallons equals 16.0 m.p.g. (17.7 litres 100 km.)

Touring Fuel Consumption (m.p.g. at steady speed midway between 30 m.p.h. and maximum, less 5% allowance for acceleration) 19 m.p.g. Fuel tank capacity (maker's figure) 12 gallons.

STEERING
Turning circle between kerbs.
Left .. .. .. 35 ft.
Right .. .. .. 36½ ft.
Turns of steering wheel from lock to lock 4

BRAKES from 30 m.p.h.
0.97 g retardation (equivalent to 31 ft. stopping distance) with 100 lb. pedal pressure.
0.83 g retardation (equivalent to 36½ ft. stopping distance) with 75 lb. pedal pressure.
0.58 g retardation (equivalent to 52 ft. stopping distance) with 50 lb. pedal pressure.
0.32 g retardation (equivalent to 94 ft. stopping distance) with 25 lb. pedal pressure.

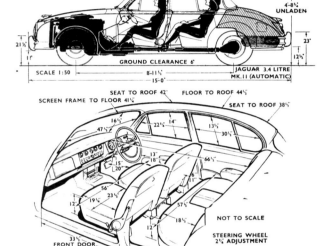

TRACK:- FRONT 4'-7¼" REAR 4'-6"
OVERALL WIDTH 5'-6¾"
4'-8¾" UNLADEN
GROUND CLEARANCE 6"
SCALE 1:50
JAGUAR 3.4 LITRE MK.II (AUTOMATIC)

SEAT TO ROOF 42" FLOOR TO ROOF 44½"
SCREEN FRAME TO FLOOR 41½"
SEAT TO ROOF 38½"
NOT TO SCALE
STEERING WHEEL 2¾" ADJUSTMENT
FRONT SEATS AND BACKRESTS ADJUSTABLE
FRONT DOOR
REAR DOOR

ACCELERATION TIMES from standstill
(Automatic gearchanges)
0-30 m.p.h.	..	4.5 sec.
0-40 m.p.h.	..	6.4 sec.
0-50 m.p.h.	..	9.0 sec.
0-60 m.p.h.	..	11.9 sec.
0-70 m.p.h.	..	15.3 sec.
0-80 m.p.h.	..	20.0 sec.
0-90 m.p.h.	..	26.0 sec.
0-100 m.p.h.	..	33.3 sec.
0-110 m.p.h.	..	44.5 sec.
Standing quarter mile		19.1 sec.

Standing quarter mile (using 5,500 r.p.m. in lower gears with manual "hold" controls) .. 18.4 sec.

ACCELERATION TIMES from rolling start
"Kick down"
10-30 m.p.h.	..	3.4 sec.
20-40 m.p.h.	..	3.8 sec.
30-50 m.p.h.	..	4.6 sec.
40-60 m.p.h.	..	5.6 sec.
50-70 m.p.h.	..	6.3 sec.
60-80 m.p.h.	..	8.1 sec.
70-90 m.p.h.	..	10.7 sec.
80-100 m.p.h.	..	13.3 sec.
90-110 m.p.h.	..	18.5 sec.

HILL CLIMBING at sustained steady speeds
Max. gradient on top gear .. .. 1 in 8.1 (Tapley 275 lb./ton)

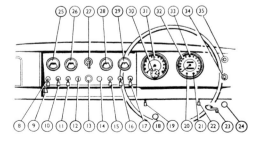

1, Heater temperature control. 2, Radio. 3, Heater air control. 4, Direction indicators switch and headlamp flasher. 5, Horn ring 6, Automatic transmission selector. 7, Handbrake. 8, Interior lights switch. 9, Scuttle vent lever. 10, Bright; dim panel lights. 11, Two-speed fan switch. 12, Ignition switch. 13, Cigar lighter. 14, Starter button. 15, Map-light switch. 16, Two-speed windscreen wipers control. 17, Screenwasher control. 18, Headlamp dipswitch. 19, Clock resetting knob. 20, Dynamo charge warning light. 21, Fuel level warning light. 22, Trip resetting knob 23, Aerial winder. 24, Bonnet catch release. 25, Ammeter. 26, Fuel gauge. 27, Lights switch. 28, Oil pressure gauge. 29, Water thermometer. 30, Clock. 31, Rev. counter. 32, Speedometer and mileage recorder. 33, Main beam indicator light. 34, Brake fluid and handbrake warning light. 35, Intermediate gear hold switch.

THE MOTOR   August 16 1961

—The JAGUAR 3.4-litre Mark 2

Power Steering and Automatic Transmission on a car of Brilliant Versatility

CUSTOMARILY those of our staff who draft Road Test Reports set out to indicate what sort of tastes and requirements a particular car can satisfy. The eight who drove this 3.4 litre Jaguar while it was on test, with others who also were invited to comment upon it, represent widely varied sizes, shapes and sorts of motorist, but the unanimity of their praise was virtually unprecedented. This model is only designed to carry four people or an occasional five, and it is only seen to best advantage on reasonably well surfaced roads, but within this frame of reference it offers an outstanding combination of speed, refinement and true driving ease. When price also is considered, it is easy to see why Jaguar competition has been driving one make after another out of existence.

From an extensive range, our test model might reasonably be described as a very good average Jaguar. The twin-overhead-camshaft XK-series engine is available also in larger-bore 3.8 litre form, or, with shorter stroke, as a 2.4-litre. Smaller two-seat cars are listed, and there is the roomier Mark IX Jaguar with longer wheelbase and wider track. Optional items on the 3.4 saloon tested included the Borg Warner fully automatic transmission, power-assisted steering and variable-rake front seat backrests.

Our first impressions were almost completely favourable. For a driver there were minor surprises, in that the starter button has not been supplanted by key-starting, and the gear selector lever is on the right of the steering wheel with the turn signal control on the left instead of vice-versa. The driving seat is extremely comfortable, however, and has an adjustment range adequate for any save quite exceptionally long legs, driving vision is good between slim windscreen pillars, and it seems easy to find a natural position for the telescopically-mounted steering wheel. Although it is hard to see the nearside front wing, the bonnet drops well below normal sight lines, and even if the waistline of the body is higher than is fashionable, one cannot complain about the size of the thinly-framed side and rear windows. After

COCKPIT of the Mark 2 Jaguar shows the walnut facia and neat instrument layout. The big pedal controls servo disc brakes, steering is power assisted and the transmission is automatic.

In Brief

Price (including automatic transmission and power steering as tested) £1,337 plus purchase tax £614 0s. 7d. equals £1,951 0s. 7d. Price with synchromesh gearbox and manual steering (including purchase tax), £1,717 13s. 11d.

Capacity	3,442 c.c.
Unladen kerb weight ...	30¼ cwt.
Acceleration:	
20–40 m.p.h. in drive range	3.8 sec.
0-50 m.p.h. through gears	9.0 sec.
Maximum top gear gradient	1 in 8.1
Maximum speed	119.9 m.p.h.
"Maximile" speed ...	113.4 m.p.h.
Touring fuel consumption	19.0 m.p.g.
Gearing: 21.4 m.p.h. in top gear at 1,000 r.p.m.; 30.8 m.p.h. at 1,000 ft./min. piston speed.	

dark, the headlamps gave long but not very wide beams.

Interior decoration is excellent, with heavily grained polished walnut on the facia and below the windows, leather upholstery over a layer of Dunlopillo, and pile carpets underlaid with soft felt. Large m.p.h. and r.p.m. dials face the driver, the latter incorporating the clock, and other instruments are central on the facia. The neat line of lift-up switches, which might otherwise be confusing, has identifications for each switch illuminated when the dim-or-bright instrument lighting is on.

Essentially this is a close-coupled four-seater body, but most people will find sufficient knee-room and headroom in the back of these Mark 2 cars, with plenty of foot-room under the front seats. The car is wide enough to seat three abreast, but as the seat cushion is very thin over the central transmission line it is better to fold down the central armrest and regard this as a car for four adults. Rear-seat travellers are most certainly not given "poor relation" treatment; an air supply from the interior heater is ducted to them between the front seats, and the latter have folding picnic tables behind them.

A luggage locker of quite generous size has a flat carpeted floor and heavy trunks are easily loaded into it. The spare wheel and tools are carried beneath a trap door in the boot. Inside the car, adequate

August 16 1961

The JAGUAR

INTERIOR TRIM uses leather, pile carpets and polished woodwork to produce a quietly pleasing effect. Rear-seat legroom is adequate rather than generous, but special provision for back-seat comfort includes hot-air ducts, folding picnic tables and three armrests.

rather than generous stowage for oddments is provided by a lockable glove box, but it would be better if the lid had a catch so that it would stay closed without use of a key. A map shelf lies below the instruments, and there are pockets in the four doors. Four interior lights, with courtesy switches on all doors, plus a map-reading lamp and a light inside the glove box, are details typical of this car's comprehensive equipment.

It may seem odd to place emphasis on the equipment when describing a model so renowned for its top speed of 120 m.p.h. but the Mark 2 3.4 is an outstanding car irrespective of price, not merely because it is faster than most others with which it might be compared, but because this performance is provided so smoothly and effortlessly by such a well-furnished car.

Most journeys start in a town, and this Jaguar is entirely at ease in heavy traffic. Modest pressure on the accelerator pedal inches the car gently away from rest, or progressively firmer pressures give graduated response until it really surges away very fast indeed. An unusual but very convenient device holds some pressure in the hydraulic braking system after the car has been stopped, until the ignition is switched off or the accelerator pedal is touched lightly, so that the car stays put on the level or on moderate slopes without any creep due to tick-over drag in the automatic transmission. The stop lights do not continue to shine whilst this device is holding the car still.

There being a more powerful engine available, it is appropriate that this 3.4-litre Jaguar should be silenced with extreme effectiveness, and its automatic transmission tuned to give very high performance (as distinct from the maximum possible) without fuss. Simply by depressing the accelerator fully, one moves away from rest without wheelspin; the car reaches 80 m.p.h. in 20 seconds and is doing 110 m.p.h. within less than 45 seconds of starting. This happens with upward changes of gear occurring automatically at engine speeds below 5,000 r.p.m., and if on some special occasion for haste the manual controls are used to delay upward changes until the maximum-power speed of 5,500 r.p.m., even better acceleration

can be recorded. This is not the smoothest automatic transmission that we have sampled; changes of gear are quite evident and alternation between 2nd and top gears sometimes occurs rather easily with small changes of speed or throttle opening, but it is very satisfactory. There is a convenient switch for holding 2nd gear in use when top gear might otherwise engage automatically, but the keener driver might prefer this switch to be combined with the selector quadrant, one position on which allows 1st gear to be engaged by the driver —primarily for braking down very steep hills.

Nobody will buy this as an economy car, but our overall fuel consumption of 16 m.p.g. (recorded in driving which was usually quite fast or in very heavy traffic) suggests that a fuel tank holding more than 12 gallons would be advantageous. The test car with 8/1 compression ratio was entirely happy to burn any Premium-grade petrol, a 9/1 ratio being available to exploit 100-octane fuel, and a 7/1 ratio for countries where fuel quality is very low. With about 12,000 miles of running-in

behind it, the test model used more oil than most modern engines.

One expects the combination of a 210 b.h.p. engine with a fully automatic transmission, power-assisted disc brakes and power-assisted steering to take most of the physical effort out of driving, and this they certainly do. Unlike other manufacturers who offer similar features, Jaguars have a vast fund of competition experience which includes five outright victories in Le Mans 24-hour sports car races, and this car goes far towards taking the mental strain, as well as the physical effort, out of fast travel. Nothing eliminates the need for alertness at the speeds which it can attain, but the driver of this car has no worries about its response to the accelerator, brakes or steering.

Hydraulic power assistance does almost all the work of steering, although servo action has been limited so that, whilst the car steers easily at a fraction of an m.p.h., it is not easy to strain the steering by turning it with the car at rest on a hard surface. For all its extreme lightness, the power steering has definite self-centering action, and although it never kicks back, it can react gently to road irregularities, letting a driver know just what he is doing. Most people felt that its gearing (four turns from lock to lock) was not as quick as they would

TAIL DETAILS include a flat-floored luggage locker which, like the rear window, is wider than on early 3.4-litre Jaguars. Rolling back the carpet discloses a cover over the spare wheel and tools.

THE MOTOR August 16 1961 85

3.4-litre Mark 2

OVERHEAD CAMSHAFTS give the 6-cylinder Jaguar engine its distinctive appearance, and in 3.4-litre form 120 m.p.h. speed potential is combined with notable quietness and smooth response for traffic driving. Accessible details include a brake fluid reservoir with low-level warning lamp, petrol filter, battery, starter solenoid, heater and screen-washer reservoir.

have liked, but with such light control very prompt response to any emergency was possible. At speed, there was no trace of instability.

Fast cornering showed no sway and only a limited degree of body roll, with a safe and consistent but not exaggerated degree of understeer. At the pressures which a fast driver should use, the tyres only squealed under severe provocation. If the front seat backrests were curved to give more lateral support, the driver would be happier and his passenger would be incomparably more comfortable during fast travel along winding roads.

It was difficult to criticize a set of brakes that did their job magnificently. No fade or squeal was encountered, no snatch at town speeds; progressive response to pleasantly moderate pedal pressures, and a tailing-off of servo assistance under extreme braking conditions, effectively prevented unintentional wheel locking. In sharp and welcome contrast with some previous cars with disc brakes on all four wheels, this model's self-adjusting handbrake would hold it on a 1 in 3 gradient in either direction—and, in spite of nose-heavy weight distribution, a smooth re-start from rest was possible on this test hill in reverse, as well as forwards, a trial which most cars fail with wheelspin.

Qualified praise was earned for riding qualities. Small road irregularities such as marking studs were smoothed out and silenced to an exceptional extent, this quiet and smooth "secondary ride" over small bumps giving a fine impression of luxury. Larger bumps were at times less well absorbed, initial spring flexibility seeming to give place to much greater stiffness for larger deflections, so that whilst big bumps encountered at speed did not produce any of the alarming effects that over-soft springing could induce, riding comfort at medium speeds is not this car's best feature. Even the high tyre pressures advised for very fast motorway cruising induced only a bare trace of body shake on cobbled town streets.

An automatic auxiliary carburetter gave prompt engine starting on cool mornings in summer, but two-position mixture strength and idling speed control did not always provide a reliable tick-over with a half-warm engine. As a safety interlock makes it necessary to select "neutral" with the transmission control before the starter button is "alive," a stalled engine in traffic proved an occasional nuisance. Once warm, the engine was a model of quiet smoothness, wonderfully inconspicuous at most times in town, but always ready with a gentle roar of real power if the throttles were slammed open. At a cruising speed of 100 m.p.h. this car has notably little noise from power unit, road or wind to spoil enjoyment of the car radio.

This Jaguar is not a perfect car; the team which is headed by Sir William Lyons and has William Heynes in charge of engineering will no doubt eventually produce something even better. In the present state of the automobile engineering art, however, what they are already making in the summer of 1961 rates as one of the best all-round cars for motoring on civilized roads yet seen anywhere in the world.

Specification

Engine

Cylinders ... 6
Bore ... 83 mm.
Stroke ... 106 mm.
Cubic capacity ... 3,442 c.c.
Piston area ... 50.4 sq. in.
Valves: Inclined o.h.v. (2 o.h. camshafts)
Compression ratio: 8/1 (optional 7/1 or 9/1)
Carburetter: Two horizontal S.U. type HD 6
Fuel pump ... S.U. electrical
Ignition timing control ... Centrifugal and vacuum
Oil filter ... Tecalemit full-flow
Max. power (gross) ... 210 b.h.p.
at ... 5,500 r.p.m.
Piston speed at max. b.h.p.: 3,820 ft./min.

Transmission (Borg Warner automatic)

Clutch: Hydraulic torque converter, maximum multiplication 2.15/1, working with 1st, 2nd and reverse gears only.
Top gear ... 3.54
2nd gear ... 5.08
1st gear ... 8.16
Reverse ... 7.11
Propeller shaft ... Hardy Spicer
Final drive ... Hypoid bevel
Top gear m.p.h. at 1,000 r.p.m. 21.4
Top gear m.p.h. at 1,000 ft./min. piston speed 30.8

Chassis

Brakes: Dunlop disc type (all wheels) with vacuum servo.
Brake disc diameters ... Front 11 in. rear 11⅜ in.
Friction areas: 31.8 sq. in. of pad area working on 495 sq. in. rubbed area of discs.
Suspension:
Front: Independent by transverse wishbones, coil springs and anti-roll torsion bar.
Rear: Rigid axle, cantilever leaf springs, trailing radius arms and Panhard rod.
Shock absorbers ... Girling telescopic
Steering gear: Burman recirculating ball type, power assisted (optional) on test car.
Tyres: Dunlop Road Speed (tubed), 6.40—15

Coachwork and Equipment

Starting handle ... None
Battery mounting: On scuttle behind engine
Jack: Bipod pillar type with ratchet handle
Jacking points: 2 external sockets under each side of body.
Standard tool kit: Jack and handle, wheel brace, set of open-jaw spanners, set of box spanners, adjustable spanner, pliers, screwdriver, feeler gauges, grease gun, brake bleeder tube.
Exterior lights: 2 headlamps, 2 foglamps, 2 sidelamps, 2 stop/tail lamps, reversing lamp.
Number of electrical fuses ... 2
Direction indicators: Self-cancelling amber flashers
Windscreen wipers: Electrical two-speed twin-blade, self parking.
Windscreen washers: Electrical pump type
Sun visors ... 2, universally pivoted
Instruments: Speedometer with total and decimal trip distance recorder, r.p.m. indicator, clock, fuel contents gauge, coolant thermometer, oil pressure gauge, ammeter.
Warning lights: Dynamo charge, headlamp main beam, low fuel level, turn indicators, brakes (handbrake on or low fluid level).
Locks:
With ignition key: Ignition switch, petrol filler cover and either front door.
With other key: Glove box and luggage locker.
Glove lockers: One on facia, with locking lid
Map pockets: Map shelf under facia panel and pockets in all four doors.
Parcel shelves ... One below rear window
Ashtrays: One on facia, two in rear armrests
Cigar lighters ... One on facia
Interior lights: 2 on centre pillars and 2 in rear quarters (with courtesy switches on all doors), also glove-box and map-reading lamps.
Interior heater: Fresh air heater fitted as standard, with screen de-misters and warm air ducts to rear compartment.
Car radio: Optional extra, Smiths Radiomobile
Extras available: Automatic transmission or overdrive, power steering, PowrLok differential, radio, centre-lock wire wheels, reclining seats, etc.
Upholstery material: Vaumol leather over Dunlopillo
Floor covering: Pile carpets with felt underlay
Exterior colours standardized: 10 (others to order at extra cost).
Alternative body styles: None (similar bodywork available with 2.4-litre or 3.8-litre engine).

Maintenance

Sump: 11 pints plus 2 pints in filter, S.A.E. 20 winter, S.A.E. 30 summer, S.A.E. 40 tropical.
Gearbox (automatic): 15 pints, automatic transmission fluid type "A".
Rear axle: 3¼ pints, S.A.E. 90 hypoid gear oil
Steering gear lubricant: S.A.E. 140 gear oil in manual steering, or Automatic Transmission Fluid in power steering reservoir.
Cooling system capacity: 22 pints (2 drain taps)
Chassis lubrication: By grease gun every 2,500 miles to 8 points, and by oil gun every 2,500 miles to 4 points.
Ignition timing: 7° before t.d.c. static (with 8/1 compression)
Contact-breaker gap ... 0.014-0.016 in.
Sparking plug type ... Champion N5
Sparking plug gap ... 0.025 in.
Valve timing: Inlet opens 15° before t.d.c. and closes 57° after b.d.c.; exhaust opens 57° before b.d.c. and closes 15° after t.d.c.
Tappet clearances (cold): Inlet 0.004 in. Exhaust 0.006 in.
Front wheel toe-in ... Parallel to 1/16 in.
Camber angle ... ½°-1° positive
Castor angle ... −¼ to +¼°
Steering swivel pin inclination ... 3½°
Tyre pressures: Front 28 lb.; Rear 24 lb. (increase front and rear pressures by 5 lb. for very fast driving).
Brake fluid ... S.A.E. Spec. 70.R.3
Battery type and capacity: Lucas BV II A, 12 volt, 60 amp. hr.
Miscellaneous: Check fluid levels in automatic transmission and in power steering reservoir every 1,250 miles.

Autocar road test 1917

566

AUTOCAR, 5 APRIL 1963

Jaguar 3·8 Mark 2 Automatic 3,781 c.c.

ONE of the most impressive sights today is the rapid and purposeful progress of a Mark 2 Jaguar on a motorway, eating up the miles in the fast lane. Like the nose of a bullet, the rounded frontal shape looks right for high speed, and the sheer velocity attained is usually exhilarating. This is the outside view, familiar to many; but what is it like to be within? Over three years have passed since our previous Jaguar 3·8 Road Test (26 February 1960), and it is time to reassess.

In the interval no significant exterior changes have been made, and the now-almost-universal sealed headlamps are the only difference in appearance for the keen schoolboy "car spotter" to identify; but many detail improvements have contributed to even higher standards of quality. Also, as a further contrast with our previous test of the manual gearbox model with overdrive, we have taken the Borg-Warner automatic transmission version for this one.

Behind the wheel for the first time, one is conscious immediately of the Jaguar's unrestricted visibility, thanks to the low waistline, slender screen pillars and the well-tailored driving position. Few cars today permit one to stretch out as well as does the Jaguar, whose adequate seat adjustment allows even the long-legged ample distance from the pedals. By releasing the twist-lock on the column, the steering wheel can be set to give the arms-extended driving position which many drivers consider ideal, while others who disagree can move the wheel nearer to them. The

wheel can be set so that it clears the driver's legs, and yet the top of the rim still does not protrude into the line of vision. Part of the curved bonnet, the lithe back of the Jaguar mascot, and the right sidelamp tell-tale are in view; but only those who are long in the body can see the left wing from the driving seat. The orderly layout of the instruments and the clearly marked controls soon become familiar.

An auxiliary starting carburettor cuts in automatically and stays in action until cylinder head temperature reaches 35 deg. C. It is adjustable for richness and on the test car the setting was a little over-generous, accounting for a tendency to stall when the transmission selector was moved

PRICES	£	s	d
Four-door saloon (Four-speed gearbox)	1,288	0	0
Purchase Tax	268	17	11
Total (in G.B.)	1,556	17	11
Extras (including P.T.):			
Automatic transmission	126	18	6
Overdrive (with manual gearbox)	54	7	6
Power-assisted steering	66	9	2
Reclining seats (pair)	16	6	3
H.M.V. 620T radio	44	12	8

AUTOCAR, 5 APRIL 1963

567

Autocar road test · No. 1917

Make · JAGUAR   Type · 3·8 Mark 2 Automatic

Manufacturers : Jaguar Cars Ltd., Browns Lane, Allesley, Coventry, Warwickshire

Test Conditions

Weather...... Dry, overcast with 10–20 m.p.h. wind
Temperature... 10 deg. C. (50 deg. F.). Barometer
29·5in Hg.
Dry concrete and tarmac surfaces.

Weight

Kerb weight (with oil, water and half-full fuel tank)
30·75cwt (3,444lb–1,562kg).
Front-rear distribution, per cent F, 57·2; R, 42·8
Laden as tested ...... 33·75 cwt (3,780lb–1,713kg.)

Turning Circles

Between kerbs .... L, 36ft 9in; R, 37ft. 10in
Between walls .... L, 38ft. 8in; R, 39ft 9in
Turns of steering wheel lock to lock .... 4·3

Performance Data

Top gear m.p.h. per 1,000 r.p.m................ 21·4
Mean piston speed at max. power ... 3,820 ft/min.
Engine revs. at mean max. speed ...... 5,600 r.p.m.
B.h.p. per ton laden (gross) 130

FUEL AND OIL CONSUMPTION

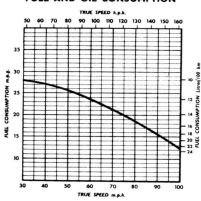

FUEL................................Premium Grade
(97 octane RM)
Test distance........................1,634 miles
Overall Consumption............17·3 m.p.g.
(16·3 litres/100 km.)
Normal Range....................16–20 m.p.g.
(17·7-14·1 litres/100 km.)
OIL: SAE 10–30......Consumption 3,800 m.p.g.

MAXIMUM SPEED AND ACCELERATION (mean) TIMES

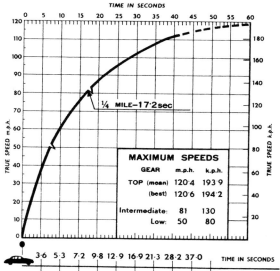

¼ MILE—17·2 sec

MAXIMUM SPEEDS		
GEAR	m.p.h.	k.p.h.
TOP (mean)	120·4	193·9
(best)	120·6	194·2
Intermediate:	81	130
Low:	50	80

	3·6	5·3	7·2	9·8	12·9	16·9	21·3	28·2	37·0	TIME IN SECONDS
0	30	40	50	60	70	80	90	100	110	120 TRUE SPEED m.p.h.
	31	41	52	62	73	83	94	104	113	123 CAR SPEEDOMETER

Speed range and time in seconds

m.p.h.	Top	Inter	Low
10—30	—	—	2·8
20—40	—	4·3	3·3
30—50	7·4	4·7	3·7
40—60	7·1	5·0	—
50—70	7·6	5·6	—
60—80	8·4	7·1	—
70—90	9·6	—	—
80—100	11·3	—	—
90—110	15·7	—	—

BRAKES	Pedal load	Retardation	Equiv. distance
(from 30 m.p.h. in neutral)	25lb	0·16g	189ft
	50lb	0·42g	72ft
	75lb	0·64g	47ft
	100lb	0·90g	33·6ft
Hand brake		0·35g	86ft

HILL CLIMBING AT STEADY SPEEDS

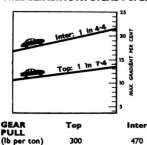

Inter: 1 in 4·4
Top: 1 in 7·4

GEAR	Top	Inter
PULL (lb per ton)	300	470
Speed range (m.p.h.)	55–62	45–55

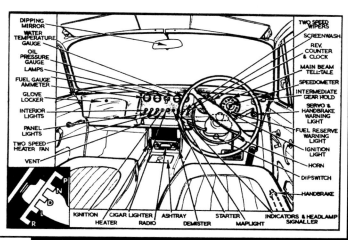

DIPPING MIRROR — WATER TEMPERATURE GAUGE — OIL PRESSURE GAUGE — LAMPS — FUEL GAUGE AMMETER — GLOVE LOCKER — INTERIOR LIGHTS — PANEL LIGHTS — TWO SPEED HEATER FAN — VENT — TWO SPEED WIPERS — SCREENWASH — REV. COUNTER & CLOCK — MAIN BEAM TELL-TALE — SPEEDOMETER — INTERMEDIATE GEAR HOLD — SERVO & HANDBRAKE WARNING LIGHT — FUEL RESERVE WARNING LIGHT — IGNITION LIGHT — HORN — DIPSWITCH — HANDBRAKE — IGNITION — CIGAR LIGHTER — ASHTRAY — STARTER — INDICATORS & HEADLAMP SIGNALLER — HEATER — RADIO — DEMISTER — MAPLIGHT

Super Profile

Left: Space for maps and small packages is provided below the central instrument panel. The Radiomobile all-transistor radio, an extra on the test car, has a retractable aerial with wind-down handle under the facia. Right: Latest seats for the Mark 2 have indented backrests to give rear passengers more knee room. Fold-down picnic trays are still provided

Jaguar 3·8 Mark 2 . . .

to " Drive " after the first start of the day; but the well-known trick of flicking off the ignition switch for an instant can be used to cut out the starting carburettor prematurely. After a night of severe frost, the engine never failed to fire at the first touch on the starter button. When cold, timing chain rattle is audible, but quickly diminishes as the oil pressure rises.

With the automatic gearbox, the Jaguar is something of a top-gear car. Full-throttle kickdown allows the Intermediate range to be held up to the governed point at 5,000 r.p.m. (74 m.p.h.) when direct drive re-engages. Intermediate hold control, within fingertip reach of the steering wheel, enables the change-down to be made on part-throttle. With Intermediate hold switched in there is limited engine braking on the overrun. In either the Intermediate hold or the Low position on the selector, the driver can over-ride the normal full-throttle change-up points. At the maximum recommended engine speed of 5,500 r.p.m., 50 m.p.h. is reached in Low—this ratio gives overrun braking—and 80 m.p.h. in Intermediate. In full-throttle take-off from rest with Drive selected, Intermediate comes in at 43 m.p.h.

General Quietness

Throughout almost the whole top-gear range the engine is scarcely heard, but at high revs through Low and Intermediate, a distinctly audible combination of induction and exhaust noise accentuates the impression of vivid acceleration. With all windows closed there is unusual freedom from wind noise at speed. This commendable quietness is not spoilt when the rear quarter vents are opened, though the front vents do provoke slipstream shriek.

Because of the smoothness and good low-speed torque of its six-cylinder engine, the Jaguar lends itself admirably to automatic transmission. Hustling along secondary and minor roads, the driver feels that he is more often holding the car back than he is urging it forward; so quickly and unobtrusively does it gather speed that it seems almost to bound away after each hold-up or corner. Similarly, the ability to overtake safely in short distances means that the Jaguar is never delayed for long behind slower traffic. Over the speed range from 30 to 70 m.p.h., it takes less than 8sec for any 20 m.p.h. speed increment even in top; and the spectacular under-half-minute time for acceleration from rest to 100 m.p.h. is a measure of the lusty performance available.

Even at this speed, there is still vigorous acceleration in reserve, and in a brisk cross-wind a top speed of just over 120 m.p.h. was obtained in each direction. A following

wind might have helped to an even higher one-way maximum, but the average for runs in opposite directions is a representative mean figure for the car, only 5 m.p.h. slower than the manual gearbox model in overdrive. Naturally this top performance calls for 1,000 r.p.m. higher engine speed than with the overdrive car, and takes the rev counter needle round to the red segment, which starts at 5,500 r.p.m.

Fuel consumption at a constant 90 m.p.h. was the same (15·5 m.p.g.) as the previous Jaguar achieved in overdrive at 100 m.p.h. Yet the overall consumption for the full test distance was 17·3 m.p.g.—a creditable figure when related to the car's size and performance, and considerably better than the 15·7 m.p.g. obtained with the manual model. The tank holds only 12 gallons, so that, within about 170 miles of filling to the brim, the winking " evil eye " of the fuel warning light reminds the driver that it is time to stop and take out his wallet again. Gentle driving is rather out of character with the car, but does offer a consumption improvement to about 20 m.p.g. fairly readily; however, it would be unrealistic to hope for better than this.

Experience of this engine in previous models prepares one for a rather heavy oil consumption, so it was a surprise to find that only three pints were used during the 1,600 miles of the test—equivalent to nearly 4,000 m.p.g. from a demonstrator which had already covered 52,000 miles. Clearly, the Brico Maxiflex oil control rings now fitted have helped to solve this problem.

At total extra cost of £66, power-assisted steering is an option which had been added to the test car. It certainly reduces the effort needed to hold the car to its line through

A pancake-type paper element air filter is now fitted, and an extra-long dipstick near the top water hose allows the oil-level for the automatic transmission to be checked easily

AUTOCAR, 5 APRIL 1963

Separate amber indicator lamps are fitted at front and rear. Twin exhaust pipes are standard, and a tiny disc brake badge on the rear bumper warns of the Jaguar's stopping power

a fast bend, against the rather pronounced understeer. Low-speed manœuvring is made much easier, and coupled with the turning circle of less than 38ft between kerbs—which is good in relation to the wheelbase—it makes parking and turning in confined spaces easy.

It is, however, a pity that Jaguar have not taken the opportunity to raise the steering gear ratio to go with power assistance; at 4·3 turns from lock to lock the steering is unusually low geared for so fast a car, and there is little response to small movements of the wheel around the straight-ahead position. The nose-heaviness contributes to good directional stability, but in cross winds at high speeds the driver has to do a lot of sawing at the wheel.

Ample power is available to help the tail round, neutralizing the understeer in fast cornering, but if this technique is used on wet or icy roads, quick reaction is needed to correct a rear-end skid. When they do lose adhesion, the back wheels start to slide somewhat abruptly, and have to be checked at once. A higher steering gear ratio would help here, too.

Excellent Suspension

Girling gas cell dampers now used in the suspension give improved control on rough roads. The springing is certainly an excellent compromise in providing the stability for such high performance, coupled with the comfort and insulation from bad surfaces expected from a car of this quality. It is especially good over humps or dips causing large spring deflections, and the recoil is damped out effectively. *Pavé* was traversed with unusually little bucketing and bouncing, while a corrugated section, which produces violent shake and vibration in most cars, was taken relatively smoothly.

On normal road surfaces, small suspension tremors are felt, as in a car whose tyres are too hard, and the Jaguar feels firm on its springs. There is little road noise, and only the occasional squeak is heard from the coachwork. The recommended normal tyre pressures to include motorway use up to 110 m.p.h. are 28 p.s.i. front, 24 rear. They may be reduced by 3 p.s.i. for low-speed work and bad surfaces, which improves ride comfort even further, but not unreasonably results in some tyre squeal in spirited cornering.

As spectacular as the acceleration of the Jaguar is the performance of its brakes, the all-disc system by Dunlop being most reassuring at any speed. The brake pedal is wide to suit those who like left foot braking with automatic transmission. In fact, there is even room for both feet together on the pedal but once 100lb effort is exceeded at 30 m.p.h., the wheels tend to lock, and 0·9g was the maximum efficiency obtained. The magnificent response at high speeds, complete freedom from fade, and the ability to stop quickly without sliding on wet or slippery roads, are the braking characteristics best appreciated. On braking to rest, a small residual pressure is trapped in the hydraulic lines which is released on initial opening of the throttle, and this

eliminates the annoying creep often associated with automatic transmissions.

An automatic transmission asset is the positive locking pawl when Park is engaged, but the latest car also has considerably improved handbrake efficiency. The sturdy and well-placed lever to the right of the driving seat now provides 0·35g braking effort at 30 m.p.h., and holds the car securely—provided the lever is pulled on really hard—on a 1-in-3 gradient, although the previous one failed on 1-in-4.

A handbrake warning lamp on the facia is sufficiently sensitive to light up, with the ignition on, if the handbrake is on one notch, and it serves a second duty in warning of any serious drop in brake fluid level.

Both improved main beam illumination and a longer throw when dipped are provided by the sealed headlamps now used on the Mark 2. Their freedom from scatter on dipped beam also make them more effective in dense mist than were the twin fog lamps provided as standard equipment. Also appreciated for night driving are a bright map-reading light at the top of the facia, shaded from the driver's eyes; an automatic reversing lamp; well-diffused interior lighting by four lamps switched on at the dash or by opening any door; and automatic illumination of both the facia glove box and the luggage compartment, when the respective lid is open with the sidelamps in use. The lever switch beneath the steering wheel for the indicators is also the headlamps flasher.

Jack and wheelbrace are clipped to the back of the boot. The boot key also locks the lid of the facia glove box. Below the floor are spare wheel, jack handle and tool kit

Jaguar 3·8 Mark 2 . . .

Jaguar owners have long had cause to complain of inadequate heating in their cars; but detail improvements have been made to the fresh-air system provided as standard with the Mark 2. The heater matrix is always at engine temperature, and incoming air from a flap vent above the scuttle either goes through it or by-passes it, as selected with the heat control. Windscreen de-icing is effective, and variable settings of the controls are possible except for the main air inlet: the flap is either closed or open, without intermediate positions. Trunking along the top of the propeller shaft tunnel carries hot or cold air to the rear compartment.

Revised front seats were introduced on Mark 2 Jaguars while the car was on test, and the demonstrator was returned to the factory for the new ones to be fitted. Their backrests are scalloped away to a depth of about 1½in. on the reverse side, to give the rear passengers more knee room. The cushions are comfortably upholstered and reach well under the thighs; but, especially when new, the squabs offer little sideways support, although they extend around the shoulders. Reclining seats, as fitted to the test car, cost £16 extra including tax; and the modified backrest is fitted whichever pattern of seat is chosen. Lack of rear compartment knee room has been a frequent complaint of some Jaguar owners, and this useful improvement is a valuable gain for those who carry the full complement of passengers.

Some who drove the car complained of the bad angle of attack to the organ-type throttle pedal, its stiffness of movement and its position well forward of the brake pedal. While improvements have been made since earlier models, these faults are not yet eliminated.

Aids to Jaguar enjoyment include an electric windscreen washer, with sensibly large reservoir under the bonnet; two-speed wipers which self-park at the base of the windscreen; a dipping interior mirror mounted on a stalk which is adjustable for length; map pockets and armrests on all doors; a large ashtray in the front console, and smaller ones built into the rear door armrests; and a cigarette lighter. Of course, the comprehensive array of instruments includes a rev counter, thermometer, oil pressure gauge and an uncalibrated ammeter; and there is a clock set in the rev counter. On the test car, it kept perfect time.

At intervals of 2,500 miles the engine oil should be changed and attention to seven chassis grease points (eight on models without power steering) is recommended. For access to the spare wheel some luggage may have to be removed to allow the trap door in the boot floor to be raised. A useful set of tools housed in a fitted tray nestles within the spare wheel.

There are competitors, both British and foreign, which can match the superb silence and five-seater comfort of a Jaguar 3·8, and no doubt some of them can also rival the vivid acceleration and 120 m.p.h. performance; but no car in the world can offer all this and still compete with Jaguar on price.

Specification

Scale: 0·3in. to 1ft.

Cushions uncompressed.

ENGINE
Cylinders	...	6 in-line
Bore	...	87mm (3·43in.)
Stroke	...	106mm (4·17in.)
Displacement	...	3,781 c.c. (230·6 cu. in.)
Valve gear	...	Twin overhead camshafts
Compression ratio		8·0 to 1 (7·0 or 9·0 to 1 optional)
Carburettors	...	Two S.U. HD6 with automatic cold starting mixture control
Fuel pump	...	One S.U. electric
Oil filter	...	Tecalemit full-flow, replaceable element
Max. power	...	220 b.h.p. (gross) at 5,500 r.p.m.
Max. torque	...	240 lb. ft. at 3,000 r.p.m.

TRANSMISSION
Gearbox	...	Borg-Warner three speed automatic with torque converter
Overall ratios		Top 3·54; Inter. 10·95-5·08; Low 17·6-8·16; Reverse 13·36-6·21
Final drive	...	Salisbury hypoid bevel 3·54 to 1 with Powr-Lok limited-slip differential

CHASSIS
Construction	...	Integral with steel body

SUSPENSION
Front	...	Semi-trailing wishbones and coil springs, with Girling gas cell telescopic dampers. Anti-roll bar
Rear	...	Live axle on cantilever leaf springs with radius arms and Panhard rod. Girling gas cell telescopic dampers
Steering	...	Burman recirculating ball, with optional power assistance. Wheel dia., 17in.

BRAKES
Type	...	Dunlop discs, vacuum servo assisted
Disc dia.	...	F. 11in. R. 11·75in.
Swept area	...	F. 242 sq. in.; R. 253 sq. in. Total 495 sq. in. (294 sq. in. per ton laden)

WHEELS
Type	...	Dunlop pressed steel disc with 5 bolts; rim width 5·0in. Centre-lock wire wheels optional extra
Tyres	...	6·40-15in. Dunlop RS5 with tubes

EQUIPMENT
Battery	...	12-volt 60-amp. hr.
Headlamps	...	Two sealed units 60-45 watt
Reversing lamp	...	One automatic
Electric fuses	...	2
Screen wipers	...	Two-speed self-parking
Screen washers	...	Lucas electric
Interior heater	...	Fresh air with two speed electric booster
Safety belts	...	Built-in anchorages provided
Interior trim	...	Leather seats, cloth roof lining
Floor covering	...	Pile carpet
Starting handle	...	No provision
Jack	...	Screw pillar with ratchet handle
Jacking points	...	Two each side near wheels
Other bodies	...	None

MAINTENANCE
Fuel tank	...	12 Imp. gallons (no reserve)
Cooling system	...	26 pints (including heater)
Engine sump	...	11 pints SAE 20W-30. Change oil every 2,500 miles. Change filter element every 5,000 miles
Automatic transmission	...	15 pints Automatic Transmission Fluid, Type "A." Change oil every 10,000 miles
Final drive	...	2·75 pints Hypoid 90. Change oil every 10,000 miles
Grease	...	7 points every 2,500 miles
Tyre pressures	...	F. 25; R. 21 p.s.i. (town and low-speed driving); F. 28; R. 24 p.s.i. (normal driving up to 110 m.p.h.); F. 33; R. 29 p.s.i. (fast driving); F. 33; R. 33 p.s.i. (fast, full load)

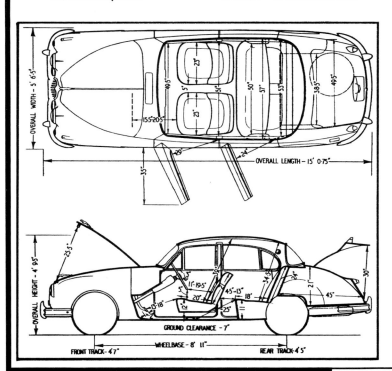

OWNER'S VIEW

Why do people buy and run Mk 2 Jaguars today? To find out, I questioned Nigel Thorley, an active Jaguar Driver's Club member and Mk 2 owner of long standing — in fact he's owned 12 in total so he should know the car pretty well!

P.S. Why are you interested in the Mk 2 series?

N.T. Basically because of my family — they've always had an interest in Jaguars. And to me, Jaguars have always been *affordable* classics, with the Mk 2 being my favourite — it looks perfect from every angle, even those silly spats look nice, it's got the edge over the Mk 1, while the later models — S-type, 420 — although more comfortable, were always "interim" models to me, without quite the character of the Mk 2. Then there's the comfort, control, quality and quietness of the car — which can still show a clean pair of heels to most of today's so-called high performance saloons.

P.S. When and why did you buy your Mk 2?

N.T. Well, don't forget that I'd had a dozen Mk 2s at various times before, including 2.4, 3.4, 3.8, in both auto and manual

forms. I particularly liked the 3.4, as it has the sweetest engine, and I've found with the 3.8 that, if you use all the power a lot, things like the exhaust mountings come away. I also wanted an early car with wire wheels, and it had to be in sound order. Eventually I found 7555 EL in 1977.

P.S. What condition was it in?

N.T. As I said, I wanted a Mk 2 that was basically good, and 7555 EL was just that — roadworthy, but getting to the point of needing restoration. Mechanically it was showing signs of age, with bad bottom timing-chain rattle, slight crankshaft rumble, and a leaking rear main oilseal. And, although it looked good 15 feet away, it was suffering a bit in the body without being a terminal case.

P.S. You were lucky, weren't you, that serious rot wasn't present?

N.T. Oh yes, rust is certainly the major problem, in our climate at least, and it's best to search out the least rusty car you can find — or afford. It saves endless work afterwards.

P.S. How much restoration work have you done on the car?

N.T. Well, the engine came out and was rebuilt, and the brakes were overhauled. As I said, the bodywork was, luckily, in good condition for its age, and I got away with two new door skins and some new metal in the front wings and rear wheel arches. The sills had been replaced before I had the car.

P.S. Rebuilding bodywork can be difficult — what was your biggest problem?

N.T. I found great difficulty in getting the proper sill/door line — you know how beautifully the doors fitted on Mk 2s originally. And you can never seem to tell if you've got it completely right until the car's painted!

P.S. Did the suspension need much work?

N.T. Not really — apart from checking ball joints and track rod ends, which you can get over the counter still, I replaced the front

sub-frame mountings. On the rear suspension I replaced the torque arm rubbers and, of course, in common with most Mk 2s, I had to have the Panhard rod mounting welded. But all the road springs are original, as my car doesn't suffer from the common "Mk 2 sag".

P.S. Jaguar interiors can be expensive to renovate — did you have to do very much there?

N.T. Fortunately the interior was well preserved — I just "Connollised" the leather, stripped and re-varnished the woodwork, and installed new carpets. That was about all that was needed, although to be perfectly honest the front seats do show many small cracks. The headlining is a bit dirty but I'm loath to work on it as it seems difficult to replace on my car which has the early sun visors.

P.S. Did you experience difficulty in obtaining parts?

N.T. Door rubbers were the biggest problem, and I still haven't got new "D" post rubbers for the nearside. Also I couldn't use ready-made carpets unaltered, because my early car has the pendant-type throttle pedal, and the carpets arrived with a slot for the organ type used on later Mk 2s. So that had to be altered. Mechanically you can get most things for the car — except for the early, notched fan belt. That was a real problem to locate! Other than that, price is the only difficulty — for instance, new petrol tanks, and the front wings now being re-made by specialists, are *very* expensive.

P.S. How do you rate the Mk 2's handling and performance?

N.T. Very responsive — the Mk 2 looks sporty, and it feels sporty. It certainly deserves a manual gearbox, preferably with overdrive — flick it out of overdrive on the motorway and there are still very few cars that can match its pull. I've never noticed much difference in this respect between the 3.4 and 3.8 either. Obviously though, you must compare the car's handling with its contemporaries — it isn't modern! Incidentally it definitely handles better on crossply tyres — it rides superbly, there are less creaks and groans, and the steering's lighter than with radials. The crossplies wear out faster, though.

P.S. Is your car in every day use — and is it practical in today's conditions?

N.T. I have run Mk 2s as everyday transport, though not 7555 EL. But I still think that the Mk 2 *is* still an economic and practical car to use — the only consideration in day-to-day use is deterioration of the body, as there are a lot of mud-traps. And, by today's standards, the Mk 2 is mechanically very simple — apart from getting at things, that is! Also I get 25-26mpg from my 3.4, using the overdrive — which I do a lot. The worst consumption I've ever had from the car has been 24mpg, so running costs are not prohibitive.

P.S. Has your car won any prizes in concours or similar events?

N.T. No — but I do take it to many JDC meetings, and in 1980 I managed to attend every single official JDC rally, mainly using the Mk 2 but sometimes with my 420G, clocking up some 3,000 miles in the Mk 2 alone. So it's an active rather than a concours car.

P.S. Do you enter the car in any form of motorsport?

N.T. No, although I see that Mk 2s are now being seen again at JDC race meetings, and that there's talk of a formula for 1957-1964 saloons in historic-type racing.

P.S. The Jaguar Driver's Club has been mentioned — are there any other clubs for Mk 2 owners?

N.T. Not in this country, as the Mk 2 Register is part of the JDC and is included in the membership fee if you have such a car.

P.S. Do you find membership of the Mk 2 Register useful?

N.T. To an extent, but there are still so many trade sources for Mk 2 parts that spares and advice are generally only a 'phone call away. However, I think the time of the Mk 2 Register will come as spares dry up, as they will do in time. The annual rally is very enjoyable though — around 300 Mk 2s take part including a number from the continent, where the car is very popular, especially in Germany and Holland.

P.S. On the subject of spares, is there any one specialist who you've found particularly helpful?

N.T. Yes — F.B. Components of Oxford, with things like rubbers, and those transparent plastic "medallions" on top of the sidelights. And Clive Eason of Ce Be Ee — he's gone to endless trouble to track difficult parts down. Like F.B. Components, he specialises in brake and suspension parts mainly, rather than major items like panels or engines.

P.S. How would you sum up the enjoyment you get from your Mk 2?

N.T. Well, let's say that the XJ is a fabulous car (I've got one), but the Mk 2 is still my favourite. On a sunny afternoon, with the windows down listening to the exhaust note, it's like an affordable XK. And, as I said before, it really does look perfect from every angle.

P.S. What advice would you give to potential owners of the Mk 2?

N.T. I'd say that bodywork is the pain in the neck with the Mk 2. Get a well preserved one, or restore the bodywork, and you certainly have a true practical classic. But do look after that body — I cleaned mine down underneath and completely repainted it, and injected Waxoyl into all the box sections. By doing that about once a year you can enjoy the car without worrying too much about deterioration. The Mk 2 offers so much it's a pity to let rust spoil it! Although everyone's more aware of "classic" cars and their supposed values now, I think the Mk 2 is still excellent value. It's certainly a great car!

BUYING

Which model?

Although we may be talking about only three basic models — and ones which look very much alike too — in fact the prospective Mk 2 Jaguar buyer has more choice than he may realise. This is because of the quite wide range of transmissions and optional equipment which was available on the Mk 2 when it was new, and in various combinations with different engine capacities. All these options can combine to produce cars of quite different character.

For instance, a 3.8 Mk 2 with wire-wheels and overdrive transmission is a considerably more sporting vehicle than an automatic 2.4 running on pressed-steel wheels — it looks more exciting and it will certainly be capable of travelling much more rapidly, thanks to the larger engine, lower final drive gearing and the absence of the ''drag'' which is inevitably present in the automatic gearbox. On the other hand, the automatic 3.4 Mk 2 is probably the smoothest and quietest of any Mk 2 (including the 2.4), the original-dimension 83x106mm XK power unit being generally acknowledged as the most balanced of the Jaguar ''sixes'' — while the Borg Warner

gearbox is free of the characteristic whine of the Jaguar ''non-synchromesh'' four-speed gearbox when its lower ratios are used. Nor, in the final analysis, will you really arrive at your destination much later than the 3.8 driver.

Of course the Borg Warner 35 unit (and especially the DG box fitted to earlier cars) is a little dated by today's standards, sometimes being reluctant to change down except when the throttle ''kick-down'' switch is used — and that can result in a rather abrupt or even jerky shift to the lower ratio. So, once on the move, most driving is done in top gear, although thanks to the XK engine's good low and mid range torque (especially in 3.4 or 3.8 forms) this is no real handicap and very acceptable acceleration is still provided. There is usually a fuel-consumption penalty for the automatic driver but, as contemporary road-tests have shown, the manual gearbox tends to encourage spritelier driving techniques which often negates its potential advantage in this respect. In any case, few people are attracted to Mk 2 Jaguars because they want to save money on petrol!

Likewise, not many owners use their Mk 2s extensively these days, but if you do intend to cover quite high mileages over long distances — a task for which the Mk 2 Jaguar is still admirably suited — the attractions of an overdrive model over the standard four-speed or automatic transmission cars are great. A healthy car can then be cruised at almost any speed the driver wishes because, due to the very high gearing of the extra gear (2.933:1), it's impossible to over-rev. the engine — even 120mph represents only around 4,500rpm, while at 70mph the engine is turning over at a mere 2,600rpm. It all makes for marvellously relaxed motoring in the Grand Style.

This is the kind of motoring the Mk 2 is best at, and over long,

fast roads it can still hold its own in terms of an effortlessly high cruising speed against most expensive four-seater saloons built today. Off the motorway or autoroute, however, its 1950's design origins become much more noticeable, with perhaps the steering being the least satisfactory aspect of Mk 2 motoring — it's very low geared and very heavy at parking speeds, which contributes towards making the car feel cumbersome when driven over twisty roads, and tiring in low-speed traffic in towns.

Although there's quite a lot of understeer thanks to that heavy old engine up front, the Mk 2 doesn't handle badly once you get used to the steering — provided that the road springs haven't sagged, the dampers are efficient, and the front suspension is unworn and the geometry correct. The Mk 2 is not a light vehicle and springs and dampers particularly tend to be hammered; the replacement of just these items can often transform the feel of a soggy car. The disc brakes you will find are good, and quite able to cope with the car's ability to gather speed rapidly between corners provided again that everything is in good order.

By now you should have a fair idea of what type of Mk 2 would suit you, and what it is like to drive. Fortunately, there are still a good number of Mk 2s around so that you will generally have a choice when you go looking for one — but take your time and don't buy the first shiny example you see. Since dropping to £400-£500 (in the UK) even for the best around 1970, Mk 2s have been steadily appreciating, led by the most sought-after variant, the 3.8 with overdrive and (especially) wire-wheels. The 3.4s fetch a little less but wire-wheel and overdrive again add to their value. Automatic and pressed-wheel cars fetch less, as do 2.4s, though in the very top bracket — mint examples with a very low mileage, say under 30,000 — the sheer rarity of genuinely exceptional cars tends to even-out the differences between automatic and manual, or engine size.

When you actually begin your search for a car, a Mk 2 in this category should speak for itself — but beware, because a lot of rubbish is talked about mileage. A car with less than 30,000 miles on the clock should look very nearly new, unless it has been abused (and who wants an abused car anyway?) Accept no excuses or "explanations" of worn seats or carpets, and instead simply ask yourself whether, if you'd owned and driven that car for whatever the mileage is supposed to be, you'd be pleased or disappointed at its condition at the end. That is a very good method of evaluating claims about mileage!

Bodywork

Even low mileage cars get rust in them, however, and the first check when buying a Mk 2 must be the bodywork. Start by standing back and looking down the side of the car to see if the doors fit properly, and that no distortion from an accident or poorly executed repairs is visible. Then start the hunt for rust by looking and feeling round the front wheel arches, and examining the wings around and beneath the head and side lights. Look directly under the grille for rust in the valance, and inside the wing where a "fan plate" and box member form the bumper support — this is a superb dirt trap and quickly rots out. At the rear of the front wings, check for rust bubbles at the top and adjacent to the closing panel behind the front wheel, which is sealed to the wing by a rubber strip. This can perish or be forced out of position by an accident, allowing water to get behind and rot out the bottom edge of the wing. Sometimes the

closing panel itself rusts through especially at the bottom, which allows water and mud into the sill and rots that out too.

Rust in the outer sill is obvious, but more important is the inner wall, which should be examined for holes or weak areas by reaching under the sill with your hand, and then pressing the vertical wall of the sill adjacent to the floor. Look under the carpets inside the car for evidence of rust in the floor itself — if there is damp this probably means there's a hole somewhere. The doors rot at the bottom, and sometimes in the middle where the loose window frames touch the outer skin via a felt pad, which, of course, absorbs moisture.

The Mk 2 can rot fatally in the rear end; prime areas to check with a prodding screwdriver are the box-member extensions which carry the rear springs, and the damper mounting turrets which are visible in the boot after removing some trim. Also, lift out the rear seat cushion and, if you find there's a lot of rust in the seat pan underneath, it may be best to disregard that particular car! Check jacking points, and all round the inside of the boot and in the spare wheel well. The skirt behind and underneath the wrap-round rear bumper is double-skinned in places and can rust badly: get the owner to take the rear spats off if fitted, to better examine the rear door post area.

To sum up, Mk 2 bodywork can rust almost everywhere and, unless you regard it as "fun", the proper restoration of a poor car is expensive, time-consuming and uneconomic. And by "proper", I mean systematically cutting-out and renewing *all* rusty metal, which takes skill, patience and quite a lot of money. There are no shortcuts or dodges when it comes to bodywork, if you want to end up with a good car. On the credit side, an increasing number of formerly unobtainable body panels in steel are now being

manufactured by specialist suppliers, including spats (steel or glass fibre), door skins, wing repair panels in various sections, and even complete front wings — *at a price.*

Interior

The interior condition of a Mk 2 is important but self-evident. Just re-covering the leather seats could cost approaching £1000 if you employ a professional trim shop, though you can buy ready-made covers, fit them yourself, and save maybe a couple of hundred pounds. Likewise, reconditioning the woodwork could cost a couple of hundred pounds, but much of that is labour so by doing the job at home you pay only for the varnish (not polyurethane), grain filler and flatting paper. Beware of discoloured headlining or torn door panels — replaceable, but at a cost.

The heat-formed door trim panels are not reproducible by hand, so look for tears or bad wear marks. At the time of writing, though, at least one specialist firm had made a prototype reproduction panel of very good quality, so this area of the car may not be so much of a problem in the future.

Mechanical components

Mechanically, the Mk 2 owner is lucky because there are very few parts which are unobtainable. However, you should still pay careful attention to the condition of the engine because of the expense of full reconditioning — well into four figures, and not a great deal less if you buy the parts and do it yourself. A second-hand engine from a breaker is still one way out of such a problem, but as fewer Mk 2s are disposed of like this now, this source is likely to gradually dry up.

Ensure that you take the car for a good run, noting beforehand that the oil pressure gauge does indeed start from ''O'' instead of halfway up the dial (!), and then reads at least 40lbs at around 3,000rpm with the engine fully warm. Acceleration should be smooth and willing, and the gearbox — though slow in operation — should not be *too* noisy in first. Where an overdrive is fitted, it should cut in, or out, reasonably quickly, and an automatic gearbox should change ratios without undue hesitation or slurring. If you can get a look at the automatic gearbox dipstick, red or light brown transmission fluid means things are probably OK, but black indicates that the bands are wearing out and that the box hasn't got long to live.

After your road test, carefully remove (with rag if necessary) the radiator cap and the oil filler cap and look for scum and frothing, which may be from a blown cylinder head gasket. On tickover, the engine should not be entirely silent but listen carefully for timing chain rattle, especially from low down — the bottom timing chain is difficult to renew without a lot of stripping down. Bearing noise, if any, should have been apparent on your test run, as should bore wear indicated by a blue smoke-screen from the exhaust.

Summing-up

Summing-up, you can see why it is very worthwhile to buy the best car you can afford, rather than a poor one with the intention of ''doing it up'' — a full restoration could cost £5,000-£8,000 easily if carried out by a professional, possibly a lot more. As for which model to buy, you've probably made up your mind already — but for sheer investment value, a wire-wheeled overdrive car must be the favourite.

Prices of Mk 2s vary widely, especially between private and trade sources, though don't dismiss the latter out of hand because if you deal with a reputable firm you have a comeback if something goes badly wrong or the car is not as described. While you may be able to pick-up a bargain from your local newspaper, most Mk 2s are advertised in motoring magazines, particularly those aimed at the ''classic'' car enthusiast. For Jaguar Driver's Club members in the UK, the *Jaguar Driver* magazine usually carries a selection of Mk 2s for sale every month.

Finding the right Mk 2 at the right money in any price/condition bracket is not particularly easy, but *take your time* and you'll end up with a real, and very enjoyable, asset.

Super Profile

CLUBS, SPECIALISTS & BOOKS

Clubs

No one can become an expert on a particular type of car overnight, and the purchase and subsequent ownership of a Mk 2 Jaguar can be made considerably more painless by joining the relevant club.

In the United Kingdom, the Mk 1/2 Register of the Jaguar Driver's Club has grown rapidly over the last few years and now has a fund of technical knowledge which any member can take advantage of — through the Register's regular pages in the *Jaguar Driver* monthly magazine, or through contact with experienced Mk 2 owners who are always pleased to pass on their knowledge. The events held by the club also make owning a Mk 2 more enjoyable, and by looking at the many other Mk 2s which attend these rallies (held at pleasant sites all over the UK) one can find the answers to questions about detail specifications and finish. Similar arguments apply in respect of other Jaguar clubs in Europe, America and other countries, where such help and mutual assistance is even more vital.

Note: Club secretaries' addresses change so, if in doubt, check with the British JDC who may be able to furnish latest addresses of overseas Jaguar clubs.

Mk 1/2 Register,
Jaguar Driver's Club,
Jaguar House,
18 Stuart St,
Luton,
Bedfordshire, England.

EJAG North America,
Box J,
Carlisle,
Mass. 01741, USA.

Jaguar Clubs of North America,
c/o Fred Horner,
General Delivery,
Holmes Beach,
Florida 33509, USA.

Jaguar-Daimler Club Holland,
Dr J.A. van Duren,
Voorsitter,
Witteven 8, 7963 RB,
Ruimen, Holland.

JDC France,
Roland Urban,
69 Boulevard Berthier,
Paris 750017.

Italian JDC,
c/o Roberto Causo,
Via Condotti 91,
Rome, 00187, Italy.

Swiss JDC,
c/o Aldo Vinzio,
BP 34-1211,
Geneva 17, Switzerland.

Svenska Jaguar Klubben,
Box 42092,
126 12 Stockholm 42,
Sweden.

JDC Belgium
30 Chemin des Deux Maisons-Box 9
1200 Brussels, Belgium.

Norwegian Jaguar Club,
Postboks 1748 VIKA,
Oslo 1, Norway.

Jaguar Club of South Africa,
PO Box 48128,
Roosevelt Park 2192,
Johannesburg, S.Africa.

Jaguar Driver's Club of Australia (New South Wales),
P.O.Box 2, Drummoyne,
NSW 2047, Australia.

Jaguar Driver's Club of Western Australia,
Steve Spark,
20 Short St,
Joondanna 6060, W.Australia.

Jaguar Driver's Club of Southern Australia,
PO Box 30, Rundle Street,
Adelaide, SA 5001.

Jaguar Car Club of Victoria,
Box 161, Ringwood,
Victoria 3134.

Jaguar Car Club of Tasmania,
PO Box 131, PO,
North Hobart,
Tasmania 7000.

Jaguar Driver's Club of Canberra,
Box 400,
Kingston, ACT 2604.

Classic Jaguar Club of W.Australia,
3 Bowden Street,
Langford,
WA 6155.

William G.Halberstadt,
Rua Haddock Lobo, 281
Sao Paulo,
SP 01414, Brazil.

Specialists

There are an increasing number of specialist suppliers who cater for the Mk 2 — usually as part of a general service to owners of older Jaguars. Most offer parts, and some restoration and maintenance services as well. Nearly all of them advertise in the specialist "classic" car press and in the *Jaguar Driver,* and while the great majority are reasonably efficient it will repay the owner to compare prices and quality, and seek recommendations from fellow owners, before deciding where and what to purchase. Few parts other than some mechanical, electrical and suspension components are now available from BL Cars, so the specialists provide a vital service in remanufacturing obsolete parts.

The following are dealers who regularly advertise services for Mk 2 Jaguars; their inclusion does not necessarily imply a recommendation by author or publisher.

P.S.W. Panels, 76a Albany Road, Earlsdon, Coventry. Tel: 0203-74030. Australian agent Bob Scott, tel: (Highton) 052-432-195. Reproduction panel repair sections inc. for wings, valances, chassis etc.

Forward Engineering Co.Ltd., Barston Lane, Barston, Solihull, W.Midlands. Tel: Hampton-in-Arden (06755) 2163. Engine reconditioning and engine overhaul kits, parts, performance modifications etc.

British Auto Spares, Saint Aarons, Usk Road, Caerleon, Gwent. Mk 2 retrim kits and materials. Worldwide service.

Phillips Garage, New Canal St., Digbeth, Birmingham B5 5RA. Tel: 021-643-0912. Reconditioned engines, spares, servicing.

Classic Cars of Coventry, Jaguar Corner, Southfield Road, Hinckley, Leics. Tel: Hinckley (0455) 613948. Mk 2 restoration specialist, body, mechanical, trim on premises. Also retail sales, some spares.

Norman Motors, 100 Mill Lane, London NW6. Tel: 01-431-0940. New and secondhand spares, especially mechanical, service.

DJ Sportscars, Swains Factory, Crane Mead, Ware, Herts. Tel: Ware (0920) 66181. Steel repair panels for Mk 2.

G.H.Nolan, 1 St Georges Way, London SE15. Tel: 01-701-2785. Extensive range Mk 2 spares.

F.B. Components, 35-41 Edgeway Road, Marston, Oxford. Tel: Oxford (0865) 724646: telex 837367. Large stocks, worldwide service.

Suffolk & Turley, Unit 7, Attleborough Fields Industrial Estate, Garratt St., Nuneaton. Tel: Nuneaton (0682) 381429. Retrimming to original standards. Export arranged.

Ce Be Ee Automobile Components, Unit 11, Holly Park Mills, Calverley, Pudsey, W.Yorks. Tel: 0532-573700. New parts especially brake, steering, suspension.

Motor Wheel Service, 71 Jeddo Rd., Shepherds Bush, London W12. Tel: 01-749-1391. Official Dunlop distributor, wire-wheels — new, exchange, rebuilds, one-offs.

Oldham & Crowther (Spares) Ltd., 27-31 Ivatt Way, Westwood Industrial Estate, Peterborough. Tel: Peterborough (0733) 262577/265021; telex 32398. Manufacturers and suppliers of panels and repair sections, mechanical and trim parts etc.

Peter Thurston, 24 Charles St., Herne Bay, Kent. Tel: Whitstable (0227) 272045 or Herne Bay (02273) 4402. New and used parts, restoration, retail sales including export.

Martin E.Robey, Whitacre Road Industrial Estate, Nuneaton, Warwicks. Tel: Nuneaton (0682) 386903. Manufacturer and retailer of body panels.

Vintage & Classic Car Spares Co., Lambert Works, Colliery Rd., Wolverhampton. Tel: Wolverhampton (0902) 55561. Obsolete Lucas electrical parts.

Olaf P.Lund & Son, 40 Upper Dean St., Birmingham. Tel: 021-622-1384 (evenings: 021-458-6641). New and secondhand parts.

Woolies, off Blenheim Way, Northfield Industrial Estate, Market Deeping, Nr.Peterborough. Tel: Market Deeping (0779) 347347. Draught excluder and trim, leather renovation kits etc.

Books

This is the first book to be published solely on Mk 2 Jaguars, but a number of others include information on the type. On the practical side, The Haynes Publishing Group publish an **Owner's Workshop Manual** which includes the Mk 2 along with its sisters, the 240 and 340, while the range of **Brooklands Books** — reprints of contemporary road-tests and articles from contemporary magazines — take in much interesting source material on Mk 2s; the relevant volumes are **Jaguar Cars 1957-1961** and **Jaguar Cars 1961-1964.** Chris Harvey's **The Classic Jaguar Saloons** published by Motor Racing Publications brings together all the "compact" Jaguars, while my own major work **Jaguar Saloons** (Foulis/Haynes) deals with all the closed Jaguars from 1931 to 1980 in considerable detail. Andrew Whyte's **Jaguar — The History of a Great British**

Car (PSL) fills in the story of the personalities behind Jaguar, while Lord Montagu's biography of the firm, **Jaguar** (Foulis/Haynes) is still a firm favourite as an overall

history of Jaguar, either in a small work at a very reasonable price, or in the original full-size version.

PHOTO GALLERY

1

2

1. Mk 2 origins . . . the basic body shape had been evolved during the early 'fifties, William Lyons using mock-ups to experiment with styling and detail. This is one such exercise for the new "small Jaguar" that was to join the XK 120 and Mk VII, and which would be called the "2.4-litre saloon". The essential shape of the new car is already there, but items like the XK 120-type grille, Mk VII bonnet badge, round sidelights and those interesting body-colour bumpers would all be changed for production. (Photo: Jaguar Cars.)

2. The original 2.4-litre "Mk 1" saloon in production form; note the XK 140-style cast-alloy radiator grille (an XK 140 is in fact parked behind this example sitting in the Browns Lane despatch area) and the thick windscreen and door pillars. Full spats enclosed the rear wheels of these early cast-grille cars, which were not available with wire wheels initially. (Photo: Jaguar Cars.)

3

4

5

3. With the coming of the 3.4 saloon, the "Mk 1" was updated with a new XK 150-type thin-slatted radiator grille, similar to the Mk 2's but without a central rib. These later cars had "cutaway" spats at the rear which could accommodate either wire or pressed steel wheels (though the spats are missing on this example which, judging from the racing tyres fitted, has been prepared for competition). (Photo: Jaguar Cars.)

4. When the Mk 2 arrived many of the 2.4/3.4 saloon's oddities had been tidied-up or eliminated; there was a wider rear track, thinner screen and door pillars, and a larger glass area. The revised radiator grille had a central rib, and the spotlamps were transferred from their outboard mountings on the bumper valance to where dummy air-intake grilles had been on the previous model.

5. Rear view of the same early Mk 2, Nigel Thorley's 1959 example (150757), showing the much larger rear window, new and larger rear light units, and the plated side window frame. Rear track had been increased by no less than 3¼ inches, although front track was still greater. Wire wheels added a further ¾ in. to both front and rear track when fitted, due to a different offset.

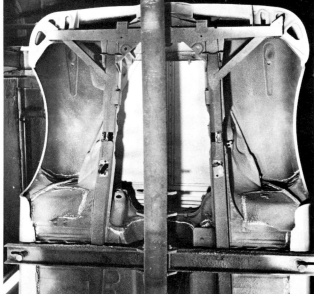

6

7

6. Internal pressings for the Mk 2 bodyshell differed little from those of the "Mk 1". This view shows the strong scuttle/front bulkhead and the large-diameter sills of the shell, together with the box-section crossmember (under where the front seats mount) which, together with the floor itself and the transmission/prop shaft tunnel, contributed much of the bodyshell's strength.

7. View of the front underside of a Mk 2 bodyshell (ignore the central cross beam on which it rests). Box-section chassis rails which run each side of the transmission tunnel and engine bay, and meet up with the heavy crossmember which forms the front bumper support, can be clearly seen.

8. Central box-section rails open out at the rear of the bodyshell to accept the cantilevered rear springs — note their central mounting. Rear end of spring was free, and pressed down on a rubber pad contained in the bracket shown, that is, it "rocked" on the centre mounting which consisted of top and bottom rubber blocks with a single bolt running through the leaves. This view also shows the inclined damper, one of the two trailing arms, and the angled, adjustable, Panhard rod. All were rubber mounted to prevent transmission of road noise to bodyshell.

9. The front suspension was also inherited from the original 2.4 saloon, a coil spring and wishbone arrangement on a heavy subframe bolted up to the shell via rubber mountings. Here, engine and suspension wait for the bodyshell to be lowered. Note the disc brakes, by that time standard on all Jaguars.

8

9

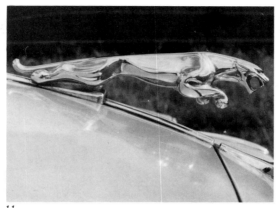

10

11

12

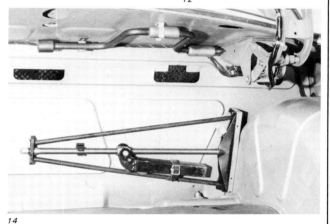

13

14

15

10. Red and gold-coloured plastic radiator badge proclaimed make and engine size.

11. 'Leaping jaguar' mascot, officially an option on "Mk 1" models, was standard on the Mk 2 except for countries (like France) where it was considered unsafe.

12. Sidelights on the Mk 2 were contained in nacelles on top of the wings; red plastic tell-tales or "medallions" informed driver whether the bulb was working, and — to settle arguments — were fitted THIS way round!

13. The Mk 2 was supplied with a screw jack with ratchet handle. Spats were removed by undoing Dzus screw fasteners which located on outside of rear wheel arch (hidden when door was closed). Rubber bung protected jacking points when they weren't in use.

14. Jack and wheelbrace (or hammer for wire wheel cars) were clipped to rear bulkhead inside the boot.

15. Luggage space was good, and bootlid was spring loaded. Floor and lid on right for spare wheel compartment was covered by a Hardura mat. SU electric fuel pump was concealed behind the wheelarch trim panel. This picture also shows the rear damper top mounting points.

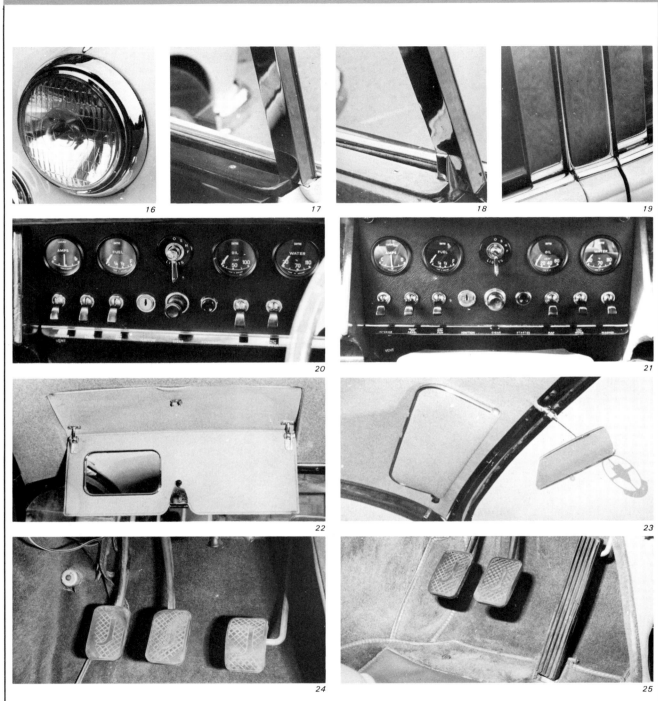

16

17

18

19

20

21

22

23

24

25

16. The following pictures show some of the differences between early and late Mk 2s, most of the change points being around 1960 after a full year or so's production had brought to light a number of possible improvements. This shows the original 'flat' headlamp, fitted to home market cars, which was later replaced by a sealed beam unit of much greater efficiency.

17. Strength of those slim door window frames was increased . . . 18. . . . through the introduction of new frames with triangular bracing at waist level.

19. The top chrome waistline beading on pillar between doors was a separate fillet on early cars like this. Later it was incorporated in the vertical chrome finisher above.

20 & 21. Centre instrument panel was originally finished in satin black paint, but was soon changed to black leather-grain vinyl because the original material scratched easily, especially where the ignition key dangled. Note also the "100lbs" oil pressure gauge on the early panel.

22 & 23. Sun-visors were originally a flush-fit into recesses in the headlining, as for earlier Jaguar saloons, but one disadvantage of this arrangement (besides expense) was that they couldn't be swivelled for side protection; hence the change.

24 & 25. Variations on the foot pedal theme. Some early cars had a pendant-type throttle pedal, later standardised as an organ type. The rarity of the pendant type means that you can't buy a ready-tailored heel mat without a cut-out in it, as Nigel Thorley (whose 3.4 provided these examples of early equipment) found out — he's having to get one especially made.

26. The oil-bath air cleaner seen mainly on early home-market and various export cars. The paper element filter as seen on the other engines pictured in this book is more common.

27. Most Mk 2s have lost this item — it's the Bakelite cover for the battery.

28. Engine capacity on all but the 2.4-litre was proclaimed on the bootlid, along with a small "Mk 2" badge on the lower right-hand corner of the bootlid.

29, 30 & 31. Three views of the seminal 3.4 litre model.

26

27

28

29

30

31

32

33

34

35

36

37

32.   Engine bay of the 3.4-litre Mk 2, a 1963 manual-transmission, non-power-steering car. Note Lucas electric screen washer in foreground, and brake fluid reservoir with Sovy low-level monitoring on other side of compartment.

33.   Front interior of the 3.4-litre. Light on right-hand side of facia warns of low brake fluid level or that the handbrake is applied.

34.   Gearlever of the manual transmission 3.4-litre saloon, with optional radio fitted into centre console. Original handbook pack is in place in compartment above.

35.   This view of the 3.4-litre's interior shows the central armrest in its down position, the Dzus fasteners for the spats and, adjacent to the bottom of these, the rubber buffer introduced after production began to alleviate door rattles.

36.   The 3.4 Mk 2 saloon, in pressed-steel-wheeled form, and with optional mirrors and wind-down aerial.

37.   This car is equipped with the anodised aluminium Ace wheel discs, which were a popular option on Mk 2s.

38. "3.8" script shows that the largest of the three available engines is fitted.

39, 40 & 41.   Three views of the seminal 3.8-litre model.

42.   3.8-litre engine compartment; no indication of the extra capacity over the 3.4 car is immediately visible, though "3.8" instead of "3.4" would be found incorporated in the block casting.

38

39

40

42

41

43. Interior of this 3.8 saloon shows the optional reclining seats . . .

44. . . . the backrest tilt operated by the handle shown.

45. Most sought-after of the Mk 2 range is the 3.8-litre saloon with wire wheels and overdrive.

46. A North American market 3.8-litre automatic, about the most popular type in that country. Note absence of fog/spot lamps; their position not conforming to lighting regulations in North America.

47. Under-bonnet view of the North American 3.8-litre; this is a power steering car, the reservoir for which can be seen on the right, below the repositioned brake fluid container.

43

44

45

46

47

48.

48.   Left-hand-drive Mk 2; centre instrument
panel controls were swopped around slightly for
convenience, the starter button changing places
with the ignition lock, and the wiper switch taking
the place of the panel dimmer switch.

49.   Cars with the Borg Warner gearbox were
labelled "automatic" on the bootlid (except 2.4s).

50.   Indicator for the gear selector was contained
in the steering column binnacle which was also
used to display the word "overdrive" on cars so
equipped. The lettering here is for the Borg
Warner DG box.

51.   Jaguar's special patented "Speed-Hold"
switch, by the operation of which the driver could
retain intermediate gear. It was discontinued when
during 1965 the Type 35 gearbox was introduced
to the Mk 2, with its "D1" and "D2" facility.

52.   Pre-1962 automatic cars had the fluid
dipstick under the central console inside the car,
but this was later transferred to the engine bay
adjacent to the inlet manifold thermostat housing.

53.   In September 1965 the Mk 2 was given the
new all-synchromesh gearbox which had a more
rounded gearlever with a chromium ferrel. This
1967 car also has the Ambla upholstered seats
introduced a year later, though leather seat
facings could still be ordered as an extra. Note the
rear window heater warning light, above brake
fluid indicator, fitted from April 1966.

54.   For its last year of production, the home-
market Mk 2 was stripped of its supplementary
lights which were replaced by US-market dummy
air-intake grilles.

49.

50.

51.

52.   53.   54.

55

56

57

58

59

60

61

62

55. The Mk 2 team of Peter Lindner and Peter Nocker, on their way to victory in the 1963 European Race Touring Car Championship. Here Lindner follows Nocker (who actually won the title) at Budapest. (Photo: Andrew Whyte collection.)

56. Bob Jane's dramatically fast (and dramatically driven!) Mk 2 fending off Brian Muir's Holden during a Warwick Farm, Sydney race in 1964. (Photo: Andrew Whyte collection.)

57. Silverstone July 16, 1960. In the early 'sixties, the Mk 2 was unchallenged on British circuits; here eventual winner Jack Sears "36" leads Sir Gawaine Baily "33", Colin Chapman "34" and D. Taylor round Copse on the opening lap of the British GP touring car race. (Photo: Tom March FRPS.)

58. The Mk 2 did well in long-distance events too; this is the start of the "Motor" six-hour race of 1962, won by the Michael Parkes/James Blumer 3.8 (no. 1) after Mike Salmon/Peter Sutcliffe led for 100 laps in John Coombs' "BUY 1". Lindner/Nocker came 2nd (second row, just to right of "JAG 300").

59. John Sparrow was typical of the many private entrants who campaigned Mk 2s; this particular car had a charmed life — originally a factory "destruction test" car, it survived a period as development hack AND a racing career to exist to this day — uncommon for either type of vehicle!

60. 1963, and more regular Mk 2 "privateers"; Mike Pendleton leads Chris McLaren round Oulton

Park ahead of Sunbeam Rapiers, Minis and Alan Hutcheson's lone Riley 1.5.

61. By 1964, the Mk 2's racing career was coming to an end; the Summers/Wilson 3.8 burns rubber but the "Motor" six-hours race of that year was won by the Alan Mann team Lotus Cortinas, which along with the arrival of properly-sorted American "big bangers", brought Jaguar's domination of saloon car racing to a conclusion.

62. The Monte Carlo rally, with all the snow and ice typical of this great event. Here a private entrant travels gingerly over ice-covered roads through the Col de la Schlucht in 1962. No major awards were ever gained by the Mk 2 in the "Monte", however, as this division of the sport never saw a proper factory team of Mk 2s take part . . .

C1

C2

C1. Side elevation of the Mk 2 Jaguar; a harmonious shape with affective use of chromium-plate on window frames and roof gutter rail.

C2. In contrast to the previous "Mk 1", the Mk 2 had a wrap-round rear window. Note plated exhaust tailpipes on this early 3.4-litre car (standard on all Mk 2s) and fuel filler flap, which could optionally be fitted with a lock.

C3. Traditional Jaguar interior trim was specified for the Mk 2; note the dark-finish veneer on this 1959 car, which is also equipped with the centre armrest (with lift-up lid) retailed by Henlys at £9.

C4. 1959 facia displays the painted centre panel with "100lbs" oil gauge, and dark veneer. Wood-rim steering wheel was a catalogued "extra" (C.25198), and so was a normal, but white-coloured, wheel. Note pendant throttle pedal too.

C5. Sun-visors originally fitted flush into headlining, and had two plated hinges and a vanity mirror. Later version was hinged from a single, side-mounted, arm and could be swivelled.

C5

C3

C4

C6

C7

C6.   The 3.4-litre Mk 2 saloon in its original
Golden-Sand paintwork, with pressed-steel
wheels. This is a 1964 car delivered in February.

C7.   Hefty bumpers were of a pattern fitted to all
Jaguar saloons from the Mk VII to the S-type of
1963, which introduced the slimmer style.
Triangular badge on bumper blade contains the
words "disc brakes".

C8

C8.   Facia of the 1964 3.4 saloon — note lighter veneer used after 1960, vinyl centre panel and organ throttle pedal. Stalks on column worked (after June 1960) overdrive on right and indicators/flasher on left.

C9.   It's the quality and aura of the interior furnishings which help make a Jaguar a Jaguar; colour of upholstery on this beautiful 3.4 saloon is Light Tan.

C9

C10

C11

C12

C10. Picnic tables which folded up into the backs of the front seats were another Jaguar tradition of the period. Legroom was adequate in the rear, but not generous.

C11. Heat-moulded vinyl door trim panels incorporated map flap in the front casing, and a pocket in the rear. Rear hingeing quarterlight and its neat little catch dated back, in principle, to the Mk V saloon of 1948, which also introduced those separate window frames on the doors.

C12. The 3.4-litre engine, perhaps the sweetest of the XK units with its sheer smoothness and powerful docility. Finish of engine bay was body-colour over sealant as this unrestored car illustrates.

C13

C14

C13.   A 3.8-litre saloon finished in Midnight Blue, a colour which compliments the Mk 2's chrome fittings particularly well. This car is equipped with radial ply tyres, optional from around 1964.

C14.   Compact and purposeful — the Mk 2 looks balanced from every angle; this 3.8 has the optional chrome wire wheels, which could also be ordered in silver enamel or body-colour.

C15. Reclining seats were, a little surprisingly for a luxury car, an extra-cost accessory. Note the earlier type of steering wheel boss on this car; later Mk 2s had a slimmer version common to the S-type and Mk X, as can be seen in other photographs.

C16. Pleasing touch on the Mk 2 was the tool-kit, contained in a rounded case which lived in the spare wheel recess. Leaflet contains instructions for filling the Tecalamit grease gun! Hardura mat has been removed to allow lid to be raised; black plate on left allows access to the fuel gauge sender unit.

C15

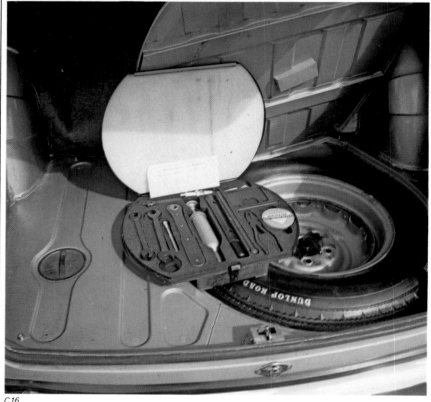

C16

C17.

C18.

C19.

C17. *Export Mk 2 — a North American specification 3.8 automatic belonging to Joe Rowe of Rowayton, Connecticut. Note plain glass (not amber) flasher lenses, and lack of spotlights. (Photo: Karen Miller.)*

C18. *The Mk 2 was much-respected in the United States, its unique blend of performance and old-English luxury making it one of the most popular of imported cars. Car number P219123 again, "P" indicating that power steering is fitted. (Photo: Karen Miller.)*

C19. *3.8-litre engine bay in left-hand-drive form, year 1963, with automatic transmission dipstick (front left) and power steering reservoir cap (rear right) clearly visible. Only the 3.4 and 3.8-litre versions of the Mk 2 got to the United States. (Photo: Karen Miller.)*

C20. *Interior of Joe Rowe's 1963 3.8; note the "plain" console of the automatic cars. Knurled ring for adjusting steering wheel reach can also be seen (standard on all Mk 2s). Minor controls were slightly re-arranged for LHD cars.*

C20.